JOHN LENNON

'The repackaging of classics is a tried and trusted winner, but Tim Coates has come up with something entirely original: the repackaging of history. He has transformed papers [from archives] ... into verbatim narratives, so, for instance, in UFOs in the House of Lords we get a hilarious recreation, directly from Hansard, of a nutty debate that took place in 1979 ... This is inspired publishing, not only archivally valuable but capable of bringing the past back to life without the usual filter of academic or biographer.' Guardian

'It is difficult to praise the idea, the format, the selection and the quality of the series too highly.' Times Higher Education Supplement

'Who, outside a few historians, knows that the British invaded Tibet? We approach these stories with an immediacy it would be impossible to contrive ... from one of the richest unexplored attics in the country.' Robert Winder, The Independent

'This is raw history ... An excellent series. It's particularly satisfying to see Goering getting a dressing down from a British diplomat.' [on **Dealing with Hitler**] **Military Illustrated**

'Very good to read ... insight into important things ... inexorably moving ... If you want to read about the Titanic, you won't read a better thing ... a revelation.' **Open Book, BBC Radio 4**

'The account is humane, moving and beautifully told. Each pocket size edition tells a good story. This excellent series makes enjoyable reading. More please.' [on **Tragedy at Bethnal Green**] **Times Higher Education Supplement**

'Congratulations ... for unearthing and reissuing such an enjoyable vignette.' [on **Wilfred Blunt's Egyptian Garden**] **The Spectator**

JOHN LENNON

The FBI files

MOMENTS OF HISTORY

Series editor: Tim Coates

London and New York

Applications for reproduction should be made in writing to Tim Coates, c/o Littlehampton Book Services, Durrington, West Sussex BN13 3RB, UK or c/o Midpoint Trade Books, 27 West 20th Street, Suite 1102, New York, NY 10011, USA.

ISBN 1 84381 004 2

Extracts taken from the files of the Federal Bureau of Investigation, available under the Freedom of Information Act.

A CIP catalogue record for this book is available from the British Library.

Editor: Frances Maher
Keying: Tricia Lord
Photographs: Cecilia Weston-Baker
Cover design: David Carroll
Design: Sarah Theodosiou
Manufactured in Singapore by Imago
Series Editor: Tim Coates

Cover photograph © SIN/CORBIS: John Lennon, 1952
Inside front cover © Hulton | Archive: John Lennon and Yoko Ono, 1968
Inside back cover © Farrell Grehan/CORBIS: Figures of the Beatles in Sefton Park, Liverpool

About the series

Moments of History are historic official papers which have not previously been available in a popular form. They have been chosen for the quality of their story-telling and are illustrated with contemporary photographs and drawings. Some subjects are familiar, but others are less well known. Each is a moment in history. A complete list of this and the associate series *uncovered editions* is to be found at the back of this book. Further details are available on www.timcoatesbooks.com.

About the series editor, Tim Coates

Tim Coates studied at University College, Oxford and at the University of Stirling. After working in the theatre for a number of years, he took up bookselling and became managing director, firstly of Sherratt and Hughes bookshops, and then of Waterstone's. He is known for his support for foreign literature, particularly from the Czech Republic, and specializes in the republishing of interesting archives. The idea for *uncovered editions* came while searching through the bookshelves of his late father-in-law, Air Commodore Patrick Cave OBE. Tim Coates is married to Bridget Cave, has two sons and lives in London. He is the author of *The Lady in the Case: The Romances of Patsy Cornwallis West* to be published by Bloomsbury in 2003.

Tim Coates welcomes views and ideas on the *Moments of History* and *uncovered editions* series.

He can be e-mailed at timcoatesbooks@yahoo.com.

The publishers would like to thank the photographers and organizations for their kind permission to reproduce the photographs in this book.

Every effort has been made to trace the holders of any copyright material included in this book. However, if there are any omissions we will be happy to rectify them in future editions.

Copyright in illustrations is as follows:

Associated Press, London – p. 82

CORBIS, London – pp. 91, 167
Bettmann – pp. 3, 5, 12, 20, 51, 52, 61, 67, 73, 77, 99, 112, 132, 135, 141 (below), 158, 160
Henry Diltz – pp. 34
Owen Franken – p. 96
Lynn Goldsmith – pp. x, 41
Hulton-Deutsch Collection – pp. iv, xviii, 119, 145, 157
John Springer Collection – p. ix
Douglas Kirkland – pp. xii, 11, 151
Wally McNamee – pp. 25, 123
Leif Skjoogfors – p. 126
Penny Tweedie – p. 58

Hulton | Archive, London – p. 23

Magnum, London:
Philip Jones Griffiths – p. 141 (above)

Rex Features, London:
George Konig – pp. 6, 17, 147
PRE – p. 107
Herbert Schmitz – p. 170

John Lennon in *A Hard Day's Night* (c.1964)

HIS MEMORY
LIVES ON

生命 LIFE
爱 LOVE

再见朋友 GOOD BYE FRIEND

JOHN
LENNON

A
MAN OF
PEACE
(和平)

In early 1975 the Federal Bureau of Investigation (FBI) assigned a handful of employees the task of handling an anticipated influx of Freedom of Information Act requests due to new legislation. Although the Freedom of Information Act had been in effect since 1967, it did not apply to investigatory files compiled for law enforcement purposes, thus generally exempting FBI files from public access.

By the end of 1975 amendments to the Freedom of Information Act had become effective and the Privacy Act of 1974 also became effective. The passage of these laws provided for broad access to FBI records which previously had been severely limited, and the task of responding to these Freedom of Information–Privacy Acts (FOIPA) requests became a very large one.

Once a file has been identified as being responsive to a request, a photocopy of the file is reviewed by an analyst to determine if any portions should be withheld under any of the various exemptions permitted by the FOIPA. The analyst uses a coloured marker to delete any exempt material, writes in the margins the particular exemption cited and has the work copy re-copied using a photocopier with a special filter. In this book exempt portions that were deleted are indicated by ***. Unfortunately, due to the condition of the original documents (correspondence, reports, newspaper/magazine clippings), some of the other passages are blurred or otherwise illegible (indicated by ---).

In the past 20 plus years, the FBI has handled over 300,000 requests and over six million pages of FBI documents have been released to the public in paper format.

At a memorial for John Lennon, London, December 1980

Contents

John Lennon as Private Gripweed in the Richard Lester film *How I Won the War* (1967)

GLOSSARY

AAG Assistant Attorney General

Airtel Urgent internal FBI communication that must be typed the same day it is dictated

Anonymous source Generally refers to usage of an illegal investigative technique

(b)(1) National security exemption of the FOIA, which allows agencies to exempt from disclosure any material currently and properly classified in the interests of national security, as defined by the current executive order on classification

(b)(2) Section of the FOIA that permits agencies to withhold information relating solely to the internal rules and practices of an agency

(b)(3) Section of FOIA that requires agencies to protect from disclosure information withheld pursuant to statute, including visa and tax records

(b)(7)(C) FOIA exemption which requires withholding of investigatory records, compiled for law enforcement purposes, that could reasonably be expected to constitute an unwarranted invasion of personal privacy

(b)(7)(D) FOIA exemption that requires withholding of investigatory records, compiled for law enforcement purposes, which could reasonably be expected to disclose the identity of a confidential source, including a State, local or foreign agency or authority or any private institution which provided information on a confidential basis

BPP Black Panther Party (black extremist organization founded in December 1966)

Blind memorandum Memo that has no marks to identify that it came from the FBI

Bufile Files located and maintained at FBI headquarters in Washington, DC

CALREP 1972 Republican National Convention (before it was scheduled to be moved from San Diego to Miami – see MIREP)

Classification numbers 100 (Domestic security) followed by case number

DID Domestic Intelligence Division of the FBI

ELSUR Electronic surveillance (includes monitoring by means of wiretapping or by microphone)

EYSIC Election Year Strategy Information Center (formerly Allamuchy Tribe, group formed in December 1971 to direct New Left activities during 1972)

FOIA Freedom of Information Act

FOIPA Freedom of Information–Privacy Acts

Garbology The study of human refuse in an attempt to divine ill-begotten truths (A.J. Weberman 'analyzed' the cast-offs of celebrities in an attempt to 'expose' their secrets.)

GOP Grand Old Party (Republican Party)

HQ FBI Washington Office

IS Internal security

Informant Regular paid supplier of information

INS Immigration and Naturalization Service

ISKC International Society for Krishna Consciousness

ITOM Inter-state Transportation of Obscene Matter

Legat Legal Attaché

LHM Letterhead memorandum; an FBI summary report prepared for dissemination to other agencies that conceals confidential sources

MDC May Day Collective (participated in anti-war demonstrations sponsored by PCPJ)

MIDEM 1972 Miami Democratic National Convention

MIREP 1972 Miami Republican National Convention

NCDMA National Commission on Marijuana and Drug Abuse

New Left Sub-category of FBI internal security investigations, referring to student and anti-war activities outside the Communist Party

NPAC National Peace Action Committee

NYO New York Field Office

OO Office of origin

O/S Outside the scope; marginal note indicating FBI's claim that withheld material is outside the scope of the FOIA request

PCJP People's Coalition for Peace and Justice (used non-violent civil disobedience to combat racism, poverty, repression and war)

PD Police Department

Protect To keep a person's identity secret

RA Revolutionary activities

Reurlet Referring to your letter

Revact Revolutionary activities

RNC Republican National Convention

S Secret — data that is deemed to cause damage to national security if released

SA Special Agent of the FBI

SAC Special Agent in Charge, or head of a field office

Sensitive Information that, if exposed, could cause embarrassment

SF San Francisco Field Office

SI Security Informant

Source Supplier of information to the FBI, usually unpaid

Sutel Submit telegram

SWP Socialist Workers Party

Teletype Coded internal memorandum, normally secret

YES Youth Election Strategy (audio-visual arm of EYSIC)

YIP Youth International Party (formed early 1968 to conduct 'Festival of Light' during August 1968 Democratic Convention in Chicago)

Yippie Member of the Youth International Party

WDC Washington, District of Colombia

WFO Washington Field Office

WPP White Panther Party (a national white, hippie-oriented revolutionary organization calling for the unbridled personal freedom of the individual)

Introduction

John Winston Lennon was born on 9 October 1940 during a heavy air raid in Liverpool, England. At an early age he went to live with his mother's sister, Mimi Smith, from whom he received a strict and firm upbringing. His two annual outings with Mimi were a Walt Disney film in December and a summer excursion to Strawberry Field for the garden party at the Salvation Army Children's Home.

It was not until he was almost 10 years old that he became re-acquainted with his mother, Julia, with whom he shared a love of music and a similar sense of humour. Julia's first husband and John's father, Fred Lennon – who spent most of their brief marriage at sea and had little contact with John – had taught her to play the banjo and she passed this knowledge on to her son. It was not long before John received his first guitar.

Between 1954 and 1956 three songs, above all, changed the face of popular music – Bill Haley and his Comets with 'Rock Around the Clock', Lonnie Donegan's 'Rock Island Line' and Elvis Presley's chart-topper 'Heartbreak Hotel'. Groups were formed by teenagers everywhere. At the age of 16, while at Quarry Bank High School, John formed his first group, The Quarrymen. One of his best friends from primary school went to the Liverpool Institute, and it was through him that John was introduced to Paul

Ringo Starr, John Lennon, Paul McCartney and George Harrison with their MBE medals after their investiture at Buckingham Palace, October 1965. Lennon returned his medal in 1969 in protest at Britain's involvement in Vietnam, Biafra and Nigeria.

McCartney, who later joined the Quarrymen. Soon Paul and John had agreed that everything either of them wrote would be credited to Lennon–McCartney – a promise they kept for nearly 15 years – and the partnership was responsible for many timeless classics that continue to inspire musicians today.

The original group changed its name and formation several times before emerging as The Beatles – John Lennon, Paul McCartney, George Harrison and Pete Best. The Cavern Club in Liverpool and especially a four-month stint in Hamburg in 1960 helped to build their success and by mid-1962 the Beatles, with Ringo Starr replacing Pete Best, had a manager – Brian Epstein – and a recording contract. By 1963 Beatlemania was born. There followed the unforgettable 'A Hard Day's Night', 'Sergeant Pepper's Lonely Hearts Club Band', 'Strawberry Fields Forever', 'I am the Walrus', 'Abbey Road', 'Let It Be'. ...

The Beatles were a phenomenon. Bob Dylan once said: 'John and the Beatles were doing things nobody was doing. Their chords were outrageous, and their harmonies made it all valid. ... It was obvious to me that they had staying power: I knew they were pointing in the direction music had to go.' The Beatles became very much the symbol of the Swinging Sixties. Hysterical and screaming mobs of fans were awaiting the group wherever they went. Already in April 1964 the Beatles had the five best-selling singles and two best-selling albums on the US charts, and they opened the door for other British groups, including The Animals, Cream and The Rolling Stones. The awards they received are legendary – from a Grammy in 1964 for Best New Artists to the 2002 Recording Academy Hall of Fame Award for 'Eleanor Rigby'.

In 1967 the Maharishi Mahesh Yogi introduced the Beatles to transcendental meditation and the following year all four Beatles spent several weeks with the Maharishi in India. Although John, Paul and George found the experience conducive to their song-

The Beatles arriving in San Francisco, August 1964

writing, they all eventually returned disillusioned – and John's first marriage was also breaking up.

In 1962 John had married Cynthia Powell – they had met at art school in 1957 – and Julian was born the following year. But John and Cynthia were never really on the same wavelength. When he met Yoko Ono in November 1966 at a gallery opening, he found a kindred spirit. They were married in Gibraltar in March 1969 and their honeymoon was spent in the Amsterdam Hilton staging their famous 'bed-in for peace'. A second bed-in followed in May/June 1969 in Montreal when they recorded 'Give Peace a Chance' with friends and visitors.

The Beatles gave their last public performance in January 1969 and the break-up of the group was made official the following year, but even before that, in 1968, Lennon and Ono had recorded 'Two Virgins', which caused controversy not only because of its content but also because the cover featured a photograph of them in the nude – the subject of one of the early entries in the FBI files.

Lennon and Ono moved to New York, 'the hippiest place on earth', in the summer of 1971 – shortly after the release of their 'Plastic Ono Band' and his solo album 'Imagine' – and soon moved into an apartment in Greenwich Village, where he found kinship with many locals, including street musician David Peel. He also took up with Abbie Hoffman and Jerry Rubin – the leaders of the Chicago Seven, the radicals accused of conspiring to incite a riot at the 1968 Democratic National Convention in Chicago. The other members of the Chicago Seven were Rennie Davis, David Dellinger, John Froines, Tom Hayden and Lee Weiner. (There had originally been eight, but Bobby Seale was severed from the case and sentenced to four years in prison for contempt.)

Lennon was soon regarded as a celebrity spokesman for the New Left cause. In early December 1971 David Peel, Jerry Rubin, Yoko Ono and John Lennon demanded a public apology from A.J.

John Lennon and Yoko Ono give a press conference in their Amsterdam hotel in March 1969, six days after their wedding in Gibraltar – their first 'bed-in for peace'.

Weberman – self-styled Dylanologist and garbologist and founder of the Rock Liberation Front, of which Lennon and Ono were briefly members – for 'leading a public campaign of lies and malicious slander against Bob Dylan': 'It is time we [everyone in the revolution] defended and loved each other – and saved our anger for the true enemy, whose ignorance and greed destroys our planet.'

On 10 December 1971 Lennon performed in Ann Arbor, Michigan, at the John Sinclair Freedom Rally – John Sinclair was a local activist leader who was sentenced to 10 years in the state prison for selling two joints of marijuana to an undercover agent. Lennon also became involved in the Election Year Strategy Information Center (EYSIC), headed by Rennie Davis, which was planning anti-war demonstrations at the 1972 Republican National Convention in Miami, and in its audio-visual arm, the Youth Election Strategy (YES).

The FBI had begun to watch Lennon closely and President Richard Nixon's aides, concerned about the growing influence of the anti-war movement, feared that Lennon might use his fame to mobilize American youth to vote against the president. Shortly before the release of 'Sometime in New York City' in the summer of 1972, Lennon's battle with US Immigration began. A 1968 conviction, in London, for possession of marijuana came back to haunt him, as under US law this made him ineligible for a US visa. He was ordered to leave America, and it was July 1976 before he was granted permanent residence.

The early 1970s in New York saw Lennon produce a substantial body of work – including 'Mind Games', 'Walls and Bridges' (in collaboration with Elton John) and 'Rock 'n' Roll' – but in 1975, following the birth of Sean, Lennon left the studio behind him and devoted himself to family life.

'Starting Over' came out five years later, shortly after his 40th birthday, and the album 'Double Fantasy' – its music portraying a loving family man at peace with himself – followed on November 17.

On 8 December 1980 John Winston Ono Lennon was shot and killed outside his apartment building in New York City.

The watchful eye of the FBI is also to be found in other titles in this series: *Marilyn Monroe: the FBI files* focuses on the time Arthur Miller, Monroe's third husband, was the focus of the House on UnAmerican Activities Committee and on the years she became entangled with the Kennedy family; *UFO's in America* catalogues the FBI records of alien sightings during 1947; *The St Valentine's Day Massacre* recalls J. Edgar Hoover's role in the pursuit of the Chicago gang of Al Capone; and Hoover's presence in Dallas in 1963 is recalled in *The Assassination of John F. Kennedy*.

1969–1970

UNITED STATES DEPARTMENT OF JUSTICE – FBI
New Haven, Connecticut

January 11, 1969

Re: Demonstration, University of Hartford, Connecticut, January 9, 1969

***, University of Hartford, 200 Bloomfield Avenue, Hartford, Connecticut, advised on January 9, 1969, that a group of students were planning a march from the university campus center to the administration building on January 9, 1969.

The march was to demonstrate the protest of the students over the suspension of the campus newspaper, *The UH News, Liberated Press*. The press was suspended by Dean of Student Relations Eugene T. Sweeney on Wednesday, January 8, 1969, after publication of nude photographs, front and back, of Beatle John Lennon holding hands with his girlfriend Yoko Ono. *** advised no march took place but a standing-room only rally concerning the issue was held in the campus center on January 9, 1969. Present at this rally were about 200 students and five faculty members. Both the students and faculty asked and answered questions concerning the suspension and other matters which they felt should be aired at this time.

The faculty felt that guidelines should be drawn for journalistic good taste, but the students refused to agree to this. When the authorities stated that no more money was to be allocated for the publication of the paper, the students stated they had been given $2,000 previously from student government funds and additional papers would be printed. A suggestion was made for a poll to be taken of students, faculty and alumni concerning the paper, but the faculty did not agree with this. It was decided before the end of the meeting that there would be no march or further demonstration.

As Private Gripweed in *How I Won the War*

CONGRESSMAN ANCHER NELSEN
TO CONGRESSIONAL LIAISON, FBI

March 5, 1969

Sir

The attached communication is sent for your consideration. Please investigate the statements contained therein and forward me the necessary information for reply.

Letter to Congressman Ancher Nelsen

January 31, 1969

Dear Ancher

Yesterday I received an album at our *** which came to me because I am in charge of the ***.

It is the latest album of John Lennon of the Beatles and his latest flame Yoko Ono. The cover of the album was a photograph of Lennon and Ono completely nude; and believe me they didn't hide a thing. It is now being sold to our young people on the record stands. Mr Nelsen, it is the most discolored and vulgar display of garbage I have ever seen in my life.

Isn't there some way we can get this album off the market?? It has to be sent in the mail to the stores, which in turn sell it to the kids. It does have an envelope over the picture when bought in the stores, so it is also fraudulent advertising. Most of the store managers do not know this picture is on the cover because of the envelope. I am at this time trying to get a hold of all of the local merchants carrying this album and filling them in on what is really on this album.

You ask why the youth of today are like they are ... this is one of the prime reasons. Ancher, I say to you, this has to stop ... and I mean now!! Please write me as soon as you receive this letter and tell me what we can do to get this trash off our youth market.

John Lennon and Yoko Ono with their marriage certificate following their March 1969 wedding in Gibraltar

J. EDGAR HOOVER, FBI TO ANCHER NELSEN

March 10, 1969
Honorable Ancher Nelsen
House of Representatives
Washington
DC 20515

My dear Congressman
I have received your communication dated March 5, 1969, along with its enclosure, a letter to you dated January 31, 1969, from ***.

A representative of the Department of Justice has advised that he is familiar with the photograph contained on the cover of an album by John Lennon.

He stated that no violation with regard to obscenity exists concerning this photograph as it does not meet the criteria of obscenity from a legal standpoint.

Your bringing this to my attention is indeed appreciated. I am returning *** letter to you as requested.

Sincerely yours,
J. EDGAR HOOVER

Note to SAC, Minneapolis:
Enclosed is a copy of a letter dated January 1, 1969, from *** to Congressman Ancher Nelsen for your information.

Note:
By communication March 5, 1969, Congressman Ancher Nelsen (Rep. Minnesota) forwarded a letter sent to him from ***. ***

stated he is an employee of a *** having *** Minnesota.

*** stated the latest album of John Lennon of the Beatles contains a cover of Lennon and 'his latest flame' Yoko Ono which depicts both completely nude.

Attorney Robert Mahony has previously reviewed the photograph contained on this record album and advised that it does not meet the criteria of obscenity from a legal standpoint.

This is being confirmed in writing.

We have had limited but cordial relations with Congressman Nelsen.

DIRECTOR FBI TO MR WILL R. WILSON, AAG

March 11, 1969
Re: Phonographic album by John Lennon
Interstate Transportation of Obscene Matter

This will confirm conversation on March 7, 1969, between Mr Robert Mahony and Special Agent Charles R. McKinnon of this Bureau.

Mr Mahony was advised that this Bureau has received a communication from Congressman Ancher Nelsen of Minnesota forwarding a letter sent to him from ***. *** identified himself in his letter as an employee of ***, which has *** in ***, Minnesota. ***, because of his employment, has observed the cover of a phonographic album by John Lennon. This album, according to ***, contains a nude photograph of Lennon and Yoko Ono. *** is concerned with the effect such a photograph may have on the youth in this country and requested to know what can be done to keep this photograph out of the hands of the American public.

Mr Mahony advised he is familiar with the phonographic album by John Lennon, which cover contains the nude photograph of Lennon and Yoko Ono. He advised that the photograph does not meet the existing criteria of obscenity from a legal standpoint and is not a violation of the Interstate Transportation of Obscene Matter Statute. Congressman Nelsen was so advised.

Note:
See letter to Congressman Ancher Nelsen dated March 10, 1969.

M.A. JONES TO MR BISHOP

March 20, 1969

Subject: Congressman Charles E. Bennett (D – Florida)
Request for information regarding proposed legislation
prohibiting the dissemination of obscene material to
minors

By letter dated March 17, Congressman Bennett sent a copy of
HR 5171, which is legislation he has introduced to prohibit the dissemination of obscene material to minors. Congressman Bennett
pointed out that his bill is patterned after a New York State statute
which has been upheld by the Supreme Court. He also sent a copy
of two other identical bills, HR 6186 and HR 7167. In his letter
Congressman Bennett requested 'any information you can provide me to back up this bill'. By letter of March 18, Congressman
Bennett followed up his previous letter with a request for 'evi-
dence' which would show that the rise in crime or the rise of sex
crimes is attributable to pornography. He also asked if we can
show that a substantial number of criminals have been exposed to
pornography. He also asked if we know of any articles or research
which would demonstrate a clear need for such a law as he pro-
poses.

We have had cordial relations with Congressman Bennett over
the past several years.

Recommendation:
That the director restrict our assistance in this matter to provide
Congressman Bennett with appropriate reprint material, and that
attached letter to this effect be sent.

XXX
XXX
XXX

FEDERAL BUREAU OF INVESTIGATION
FOIPA DELETED PAGE INFORMATION SHEET

207 Page(s) withheld entirely at this location in the file. One or more of the following statements, where indicated, explain this deletion.

☒ Deleted under exemption(s) _(b)(7)(c)_ with no segregable material available for release to you.

☐ Information pertained only to a third party with no reference to you or the subject of your request.

☐ Information pertained only to a third party. Your name is listed in the title only.

☐ Documents originated with another Government agency(ies). These documents were referred to that agency(ies) for review and direct response to you.

____ Pages contain information furnished by another Government agency(ies). You will be advised by the FBI as to the releasability of this information following our consultation with the other agency(ies).

____ Page(s) withheld for the following reason(s):

_____

_____

☐ For your information: _____

_____

☒ The following number is to be used for reference regarding these pages:
   _9-63510_   _(ENTIRE FILE)_   _HEADQUARTERS_

THE VILLAGE VOICE – DECEMBER 25, 1969

I was in Toronto last week to do an interview for WABC–FM with John and Yoko Ono Lennon: one of the reasons the Lennons were there, as you probably already know, was to announce their 'peace festival'.

It seems everyone and his greedy brother is slapping together a rock festival, but this one sounds like it might headline the summer's fare, and include one unique and cosy feature. The entire stage will be in the form of a massive bed, and so this July 3, 4, and 5 the joyful noise of 'rock, peace poetry, and whatever' will be coming from between the sheets. Then the Lennons would like to tuck the whole package in and take it on a world tour, especially to Russia and Czechoslovakia.

When I asked him about the Beatles as an entity, John said casually that they might never play again, then added they feel that way every time they finish an album. On the other hand, he mentioned that it is getting increasingly hard to fit all their songs on one LP, notably since George has begun to write so prolifically. He did seem sure they would never tour again as a group. As for music, John felt they hadn't made any dynamic changes since 'Sergeant Pepper', and their music should go further out again. He also denied that the Beatles are leaving the Allan Klein management, and in fact said he liked Klein, not only as a businessman but also as a person.

When asked why he comes to Canada so often, other than problems with his US visa, John answered, 'Because it talks to China'. Another reason why he was there this time was to sign the 5,000 copies of his erotic lithographs. In between writer's cramp and macrobiotic meals (served by two chefs flown in from the Caldron on the Lower East Side), the Lennons planned the next

Manhattan, New York, December 1969: One of several large billboards purchased in 11 major world cities to display the Lennons' Christmas message for peace

phases of their peace campaign. They just completed their bill-
board event in Times Square and 10 other major cities, and will
present another surprise --- in the next few weeks.

Both John and Yoko seem unaffected that war is even more
powerful a --- now, despite all their love flutter and commotion.
'We believe in selling peace ... nobody says to give up Christianity
because Christ died.'

Their latest single will be a 'peace poll'. Letters, postcards, or
any other voucher from the peace-bent will be sent to a prescribed
– as yet to be announced – address. They think that maybe a
mountain of this mail can be delivered to one of those ministers
of war who is impressed by statistics.

John Lennon, November 1963

WJWL RADIO TO THE ROYAL CANADIAN MOUNTED POLICE, MONTREAL

March 18, 1970

WJWL has been approached by the Peace Station Network of 120 Avenue Road, Toronto 5, Ontario, Canada, to participate in a network of stations broadcasting 5-minute 'peace' programs.

On a WJWL telephone listener opinion program, I solicited response as to whether WJWL should or should not air the 'peace' programs. The response was overwhelmingly against such programming. I advised the Peace Station Network to remove WJWL and our FM affiliate, WSEA, from their mailing lists.

I was subsequently approached by a youth delegation with petition in hand claiming the station was unfair in refusal of time. We were abrogating the constitutional guarantee of freedom of expression. I tried to explain that this was a Canadian organization, with no claim to any US rights. Not satisfied, they claimed it was 'their right to hear' that I was infringing on. Well, to head off any prolonged debate, I agreed to listen to a tape from the Peace Station Network people if they would procure one. After so reviewing same, we would make a final judgement.

The purpose of this letter is to ascertain if the Royal Canadian Mounted Police has any information which may shed some light on the Peace Station Network. I would like to know who the officers are; what their purposes are; how they are financed; and why the Canadian base. I have my suspicions. The decision of course is mine. I would appreciate, however, something more concrete than my intuition to support whatever that decision may be.

EDWARD MARZOA
Manager

ALL CORRESPONDENCE TO
BE ADDRESSED:
THE COMMISSIONER
ROYAL CANADIAN MOUNTED POLICE
OTTAWA 7, CANADA

HEADQUARTERS – DIRECTION GÉNÉRALE

TOUTE CORRESPONDANCE
ÊTRE ADRESSÉE COMME
LE COMMISSAIRE
GENDARMERIE ROYALE DU
OTTAWA 7, CANAD

OTTAWA 7, CANADA

YOUR NO.
VOTRE N°

OUR NO.
NOTRE N°　██████████ (670)

April 21, 1970.

The deletions on this document were made at the request of the Canadian Security Intelligence Service.

<u>CONFIDENTIAL</u>

Mr. Moss Lee Innes,
c/o U.S. Embassy,
Ottawa, Ontario.

Dear Sir:

Attached is a copy of a letter dated March 18, 1970 which was received from Mr. Edward MARZOA of Radio Station WJWL in <u>Georgetown, Delaware</u> and a copy of our reply to Mr. MARZOA dated April 21, 1970.

2.　According to the February 20, 1970 edition of the <u>Telegram</u> (Toronto daily newspaper), Mr. Ritchie YORKE of Toronto, Ontario was endeavouring to set up a "Peace Network", being a loose organization of radio stations aimed at promoting the July 3/5, 1970 Mosport Peace Festival at Mosport, Ontario. ██████████ *CANADA*

3.　The Mosport Peace Festival was initiated by John LENNON (of Beatle fame) and his wife, while visiting Canada during December 1969. To facilitate the "peace festival", which in fact would be a youth orientated rock festival, Ritchie YORKE and John BROWER ██████████ both of Toronto, Ontario, were engaged as advertising and expediting co-ordinators for promotion of the "festival". The Mosport location for the "festival" was recently vetoed by the Ontario Municipal Board and at the present time it is not certain whether the "festival" will proceed at some other location. *CANADA*

4.　Should Mr. MARZOA contact your Agency, you may verbally pass the information contained in paragraphs 2 and 3 to him.

Yours truly,

(J.E.M. Barrette),
Assistant Commissioner,
Director,
Security and Intelligence.

ROYAL CANADIAN MOUNTED POLICE, OTTAWA TO US EMBASSY, OTTAWA

April 21, 1970
Mr Moss Lee Innes
c/o US Embassy
Ottawa, Ontario

Attached is a copy of a letter dated March 16, 1970, which was received from Mr Edward Marzoa of Radio Station WJWL in Georgetown, Delaware, and a copy of our reply to Mr Marzoa dated April 21, 1970.

According to the February 20, 1970, edition of the *Telegram* (Toronto daily newspaper), Mr Ritchie Yorke of Toronto, Ontario, was endeavouring to set up a 'Peace Network', being a loose organization of radio stations aimed at promoting the July 3/5, 1970, Mosport Peace Festival at Mosport, Ontario. ★★★

The Mosport Peace Festival was initiated by John Lennon (of Beatle fame) and his wife while visiting Canada during December 1969. To facilitate the 'peace festival', which in fact would be a youth-orientated rock festival, Ritchie Yorke and John Brower ★★★, both of Toronto, Ontario, were engaged as advertising and expediting coordinators for promotion of the 'festival'. The Mosport location for the 'festival' was recently vetoed by the Ontario Municipal Board, and at the present time it is not certain whether the 'festival' will proceed at some other location.

Should Mr Marzoa contact your Agency, you may verbally pass the information contained in paragraphs 2 and 3 to him.

J.E.M.BARRETTE
Assistant Commissioner
Director, Security and Intelligence

ROYAL CANADIAN MOUNTED POLICE, OTTAWA TO RADIO STATION WJWL

April 21, 1970
Mr Edward Marzoa
Radio Station WJWL
Georgetown, Delaware

Dear Sir

This will acknowledge receipt of your letter dated March 18, 1970, concerning the lobbying of a youth delegation under the auspices of 'Peace Station Network' of 120 Avenue Road, Toronto 5, Ontario, for the purpose of having WJWL broadcast 5-minute 'peace' programs.

We regret that we are unable to supply you with the information which you requested, as government policy requires us to liaise with the Federal Bureau of Investigation in matters related to enquiries of this nature. We therefore suggest you redirect your enquiry to the Federal Bureau of Investigation.

Yours truly,

S.V.M.CHISHOLM
Superintendent

AIRTEL
DIRECTOR FBI TO SACs NEW YORK AND LOS ANGELES

April 23, 1970
Re: John Lennon
     George Harrison
     Patricia Harrison
     Information concerning ***

On April 22, 1970, a representative of the Department of State advised that the American Embassy in London had submitted information showing the captioned individuals planned to depart from London, England, on April 23, 1970, via TWA Flight 761, which will arrive in Los Angeles at 7.15 local time. These individuals are affiliated with the Beatles musical group and Lennon will be travelling under the name Chambers while the Harrisons are using the name Masters.

Lennon and the Harrisons will remain in Los Angeles until May 6, 1970, for business discussions with Capital Records and other enterprises. They will travel to New York City on May 7, 1970, for further business discussions and will return to London on or about May 16, 1970. Waivers were granted by the Immigration and Naturalization Service, and the Embassy was to issue visas on April 22, 1970. In this case waivers were necessary in view of the ineligibility of these three individuals to enter the US due to their reputations in England as narcotic users.

While Lennon and the Harrisons have shown no propensity to become involved in violent anti-war demonstrations, each recipient remain alert for any information of such activity on their part or for information indicating they are using narcotics. Submit any pertinent information obtained in form suitable for dissemination.

Memorandum

TO : DIRECTOR, FBI DATE: 8/4/70
ATTN: LIAISON SECTION

FROM : SAC, LOS ANGELES (163-1854) (RUC)

SUBJECT: ███████ aka

b7c FPC ███████

OO: Bureau

☒ REMAINS UNCLASSIFIED
9320 2/24/81

Re Bureau airtel to Los Angeles dated 7/30/70, and Los Angeles teletype to the Bureau dated 8/3/70.

Enclosed for the Bureau are six copies of a LHM dated and captioned as above.

All investigation in this matter was conducted by SA ███████████ unless otherwise indicated.

SA ████████ contacted ██████████ (source), ███████████████ and ████████

First source is ██████████ Due to nature of information furnished by this source, it is not being classified. Second source is ████████ who was contacted by SA ███████████████ Third source is ████████████████ who was contacted by SA ███████████ Fourth source is ████████████ who was also contacted by SA ████████

All sources furnishing information had no objections to the information they furnished being disseminated to a foreign government.

Information furnished by second source advised that International Society for Krishna Consciousness (ISKC) was backed by GEORGE HARRISON and JOHN LENNON, not further identified. It appears these individuals are members of the Beatles singing group who reside in England.

No further investigation is being conducted by Los Angeles in this matter.

2 - Bureau (Encls. 6) (AM - REGISTERED)
2 - Los Angeles
kaf
(4) OFFICE COPY

SAC LOS ANGELES TO DIRECTOR FBI

August 4, 1970
Subject: *** aka ***

Re Bureau airtel to Los Angeles dated July 30, 1970, and Los Angeles teletype to the Bureau dated August 3, 1970.

Enclosed for the Bureau are six copies of a LHM dated and captioned as above.

All investigation in this matter was conducted by SA *** unless otherwise indicated.

SA *** contacted *** (source), *** and ***.

First source is ***. Due to nature of information furnished by this source, it is not being classified. Second source is ***, who was contacted by SA ***. Third source is ***, who was contacted by SA ***. Fourth source is ***, who was also contacted by SA ***.

All sources furnishing information had no objections to the information they furnished being disseminated to a foreign government.

Information furnished by second source advised that International Society for Krishna Consciousness (ISKC) was backed by George Harrison and John Lennon, not further identified. It appears these individuals are members of the Beatles singing group who reside in England.

No further investigation is being conducted by Los Angeles in this matter.

*** ALSO KNOWN AS ***

'Sum and substance of Krishna is chanting name of Supreme Being.' Romance and conventional courting is frowned upon. The spirit master in each city chooses mates for members. Members of

ISKC do not partake in drugs, intoxicants, meat, fish, eggs, gambling or illicit sex life. Their chants are kept track of on a string of 108 beads which they repeat 16 times daily. Funds are obtained by ISKC members by begging and selling incense.

On August 3, 1970, a second source, who has furnished reliable information in the past, furnished the following information:

The branch manager of ISKC is Gregory Scharf, who employs 75 people in Los Angeles, California. Headquarters of ISKC is 3840 North Beacon Street, Boston, Massachusetts. ISKC is backed by George Harrison and John Lennon (not further described). Assets of ISKC in Los Angeles are $250,000, and this group is described as a 'meditation group'.

Files of the Los Angeles Office of the FBI disclosed no information regarding Gregory Scharf.

On August 3, 1970, a third source, who has furnished reliable information in the past, furnished the following information:

The Beach Boys is a popular musical and recording group similar to the Beatles. The Beach Boys formerly enjoyed tremendous financial success, but current popularity has diminished. The Beatles and Beach Boys were interested in the philosophy of India and support the same spiritual leader, Maharishi Mahesh Yogi.

1971

DYLAN AND WEBERMAN: A LETTER
The Village Voice, December 2, 1971

We ask A.J. Weberman to publicly apologize to Bob Dylan for leading a public campaign of lies and malicious slander against Dylan in the past year. It is about time someone came to Dylan's defense when A.J. published articles and went on radio calling Dylan a junkie – which he never was –, attacked Dylan for 'deserting the movement' – when he was there before the movement and helped create it – and publicized Dylan's address and phone – exposing Bob and his wife and children to public embarrassment and abuse.

Dylan is more than a myth – he is a human being, like you and me. He has feelings and sensitivities like you and me. Who is there among us who has not had his consciousness shaped by the words and music of Bob Dylan? Yet who raised his or her voice or uttered a word to defend Dylan when A.J. Weberman began his personal campaign of slander against Dylan – in the true tradition of the sensationalistic press willing to print anything about someone famous – even organizing demonstrations at Dylan's home – for god's sake: can't Dylan have some privacy! Can't he have some peace of mind in his own home to think and write and make music and be with his family?

Weberman took advantage of Dylan's fame. If Bob Dylan attacked A.J. Weberman, who would listen or publish it? If A.J. Weberman has some 'inside gossip' or 'the real truth' about Bob Dylan, everyone is all ears because everyone wants to talk about Bob Dylan. Stories spread from person to person in an ever-widening circle of exaggeration and bullshit. No one cares to find out the truth about Bob Dylan, the person. They are too busy amusing themselves by telling outlandish stories about Bob Dylan – the myth – whom they have never met.

Bob Dylan and George Harrison performing at a concert for Bangladesh, Madison Square Garden, New York, August 1971

Dylan and Weberman: A Letter

WE ASK A. J. Weberman to publicly apologize to Bob Dylan for leading a public campaign of lies and malicious slander against Dylan in the past year. It is about time someone came to Dylan's defense when A. J. published articles and went on radio calling Dylan a junkie—which he never was—attacked Dylan for "deserting the movement"—when he was there before the movement and helped create it—and publicized Dylan's address and phone—exposing Bob and his wife and children to public embarrassment and abuse.

Dylan is more than a myth—he is a human being, like you and me. He has feelings and sensitivities like you and me. Who is there among us who has not had his consciousness shaped by the words and music of Bob Dylan? Yet who raised his or her voice or uttered a word to defend Dylan when A. J. Weberman began his personal campaign of slander against Dylan—in the true tradition of the sensationalistic press willing to print anything about someone famous—even organizing demonstrations at Dylan's home—for god's sake:—can't Dylan have some privacy! Can't he have some peace of mind in his own home to think and write and make music and be with his family?

Weberman took advantage of Dylan's fame. If Bob Dylan attacked A. J. Weberman, who would listen or publish it? If A. J. Weberman has some "inside gossip" or "the real truth" about Bob Dylan, everyone is all ears because everyone wants to talk about Bob Dylan. Stories spread from person to person in an ever-widening circle of exaggeration and bullshit. No one cares to find out the truth about Bob Dylan, the person. They are too busy amusing themselves by telling outlandish stories about Bob Dylan—the myth—whom they have never met.

Weberman tried to make a name for himself by attacking Dylan and proclaiming himself a Dylanologist or something like that. No one else named Weberman an expert on Dylan. Weberman calls himself an expert, and all of a sudden the press is all over him trying to get information or gossip about Dylan. Now whenever someone writes about Bob Dylan, they also interview A. J. because he is a self-proclaimed authority on Dylan's music. A. J. claims everything Dylan writes is either about Weberman or about heroin. What bullshit!

Weberman is to Dylan as Manson is to the Beatles—and Weberman uses what he interprets from Dylan's music to try and kill Dylan and build his own fame. Now A. J. Weberman takes credit for Dylan's "George Jackson" song. More egocentric bullshit. Dylan wrote in spite of Weberman and in spite of "the movement." Dylan wrote it because he felt it.

A. J. Weberman's campaign—and the movement's complicity in it—is in the current fad of everyone in the revolution attacking each other and spreading false rumors about each other. It's time we defended and loved each other—and saved our anger for the true enemy, whose ignorance and greed destroys our planet.

—The Rock Liberation Front:
David Peel, Jerry Rubin,
Yoko Ono, John Lennon

Rock Demonstration

The Rock Liberation Front will demonstrate on Friday, December 3, from 1.30 to 3.30 p. m. against Capitol Records at their offices at 1370 Sixth Avenue (at 56th Sreet) to protest Capitol's refusal to press the Madison Square Garden Bangla Desh benefit concert at cost, so that all profits from the disc can go directly to Pakistani refugees in India. Another purpose of the demonstration is to stop Capitol from suing and/or getting an injunction against any other record company that agrees to press it at cost. For information call 477-6243.

Weberman tried to make a name for himself by attacking Dylan and proclaiming himself a Dylanologist or something like that. No one else named Weberman an expert on Dylan. Weberman calls himself an expert, and all of a sudden the press is all over him trying to get information or gossip about Dylan. Now whenever someone writes about Bob Dylan, they also interview A.J. because he is a self-proclaimed authority on Dylan's music. A.J. claims everything Dylan writes is either about Weberman or about heroin. What bullshit.

Weberman is to Dylan as Manson is to the Beatles – and Weberman uses what he interprets from Dylan's music to try and kill Dylan and build his own fame. Now A.J. Weberman takes credit for Dylan's 'George Jackson' song. More egocentric bullshit. Dylan wrote it in spite of Weberman and in spite of 'the movement'. Dylan wrote it because he felt it.

A.J. Weberman's campaign – and the movement's complicity in it – is in the current fad of everyone in the revolution attacking each other and spreading false rumors about each other. It is time we defended and loved each other – and saved our anger for the true enemy, whose ignorance and greed destroys our planet.

The Rock Liberation Front:
David Peel, Jerry Rubin,
Yoko Ono, John Lennon

ROCK DEMONSTRATIONS
The Village Voice, December 2, 1971

The Rock Liberation Front will demonstrate on Friday December 3, from 1.30 to 3.30 p.m. against Capitol Records at their offices at 1370 Sixth Avenue (at 56th Street) to protest Capitol's refusal to press the Madison Square Garden Bangla Desh benefit concert at cost, so that all profits from the disc can go directly to Pakistani refugees in India. Another purpose of the demonstration is to stop Capitol from suing and/or getting an injunction against any other record company that agrees to press it at cost. For information call 477-6243.

LENNON LET HIS FOLLOWERS DOWN
The Detroit News, December 13, 1971

If anyone went to the John Sinclair rally Friday night in Ann Arbor for the sole purpose of seeing a rare John Lennon performance, he had to go away disappointed.

Lennon was the drawing card that brought many, if not most, of the 15,000 young people to Crisler Arena.

But almost eight hours of speeches by medical leaders, poetry by Allen Ginsberg, country rock by Commander Cody and rhythm and blues by Stevie Wonder preceded the former Beatle's appearance.

When he did, it was brief, and one major factor nearly spoiled the whole thing.

He brought Yoko Ono.

Mrs Lennon may be the genius that John keeps insisting she is. Possibly, if he keeps heavily hyping her, someone might believe it.

But before a singer can be judged, she must first be able to carry a tune. Yoko can't even remain on key.

This was evidenced clearly when she sang 'O Sisters, O Sisters', a Women's Lib tune she claimed she wrote for the 'Sisters of Ann Arbor' the day before the rally.

Standing beside her, Lennon managed not to wince. He even kissed her when it was over.

Lennon's portion of the show was hardly worth the wait – three songs, all of which were unfamiliar to the crowd.

They were so new that Lennon had to read the lyrics from a music stand as he sang.

His tribute to Sinclair, which began 'John Sinclair, in the stir for breathing air', was played on steel guitar.

Because of the name attached to it, the song probably will become a million seller and should make Detroit Recorder's Court Judge Robert J. Colombo an anti-hero in the subculture. ('He gave him (Sinclair) 10 (years) for two (marijuana cigarets), what else can Judge Colombo do?')

It was an interesting piece, but lacking Lennon's usual standards.

Lennon and Yoko were dressed in matching black leather jackets, unzipped to reveal 'Free John Now' T-shirts. Lennon wore small circular sunglasses. He was flippant and tried to give the crowd the impression that they weren't watching a superstar, but simply the working-class hero.

Preceding the Lennon's were David Peel and the Lower East Side: positively the worst act I've ever seen. The greasy-looking Peel sang like a deranged gorilla. The lyrics of one song consisted solely of repeating 'mara-wanna' about 50 times.

The best rock 'n' roll of the evening was provided by some local artists. Bob Seger (formerly with the System) and Teegarden and VanWinkle combined for the evening's musical highlight.

Seger's 'Looking Back' may be only a four-chord progression piece, but it's well performed and the lyrics should go down as the subculture's national anthem.

BILL GRAY
Amusement Writer

John Lennon and Yoko Ono performing in 1973

CONFIDENTIAL

UNITED STATES GOVERNMENT

Memorandum

TO : SAC DETROIT ████████ 62,670 (ⓧ(u)) DATE: 12/23/71 b7D

FROM : SA ████████ b7C (ⓧ(u))

SUBJECT: ████████ 62 (ⓧ(u)) b7D

FOI/PA

TE	CI	SI		E	
PC	PCI	PSI		E (Prob)	
				E (Ghett...)	

Dates of Contact — DO NOT DESTROY SERIAL

12/14/71 — PRIOR TO

File #s on which contacted (Use Titles if File #s not available or when CI provides positive information)

b7C ████████ ████████

157-3075 RPP (ⓧ(u))
b7C ████████

100-0 JOHN LENNON (Info concerning)
100-36217 WPP (RAINBOW PEOPLE'S PARTY, Ann Arbor Chapter)
100-37957 WPP (RAINBOW PEOPLE'S PARTY, Detroit Chapter)

Purpose and results of contact

☐ NEGATIVE
☒ POSITIVE
☐ STATISTIC

Informant advised that he attended the rally held in Ann Arbor on 12/10/71 to raise funds for the release of JOHN SINCLAIR from prison. Informant drove to Ann Arbor with ████████ (name unknown). Upon arriving at Ann Arbor, they met three white males and two white females (names not recalled). The individuals whom they met seemed to know a lot of people and took informant behind the podium to meet BOBBY SEALE, as he was finishing his speech. (ⓧ(u))

SEALE greeted them as "brothers in the movement". Informant advised that SEALE was wearing a very expensive diamond ring and a watch that he estimated as costing at least $1,000.00. When SEALE gave his public speech or met the public he turned the diamond ring around so that the stones could not be seen. SEALE told the informant and others in the group with him that the RPP is opening three food clinics and that...

Has informant shown any indication of emotional instability, unreliability or furnishing false information? No

☒ Informant certified that he has furnished all information obtained by him since last contact.

PERSONAL DATA

Coverage Security

100-0 - 46 18

1 - ████████ 1 - 157-3075
1 - ████████ 1 - 100-0
1 - 100-37957 1 - 100-36217

CONFIDENTIAL

MEMORANDUM – UNITED STATES GOVERNMENT
SA *** TO SAC DETROIT ***

December 23, 1971
Subject: ***
Dates of contact: December 14, 1971
Files on which contacted: ***

<blockquote>

Rainbow People's Party (RPP)

John Lennon (Info concerning)

WPP (Rainbow People's Party, Ann
Arbor Chapter)

WPP (Rainbow People's Party,
Detroit Chapter)

</blockquote>

Informant advised that he attended the rally held in Ann Arbor on December 10, 1971, to raise funds for the release of John Sinclair from prison. Informant drove to Ann Arbor with *** (name unknown). Upon arriving at Ann Arbor, they met three white males and two white females (names not recalled). The individuals whom they met seemed to know a lot of people and took informant behind the podium to meet Bobby Seale, as he was finishing his speech.

Seale greeted them as 'brothers in the movement'. Informant advised that Seale was wearing a very expensive diamond ring and a watch that he estimated as costing at least $1,000.00. When Seale gave his public speech or met the public he turned the diamond ring around so that the stones could not be seen. Seale told the informant and others in the group with him that the RPP is opening three food clinics and that: 'If the pigs interfere with him in any way, he will open free gun clinics and distribute free guns.' Seale elaborated on this point and said: 'We have access to all the guns we want, and we'll kill any "pig" that gives us trouble.'

Informant noticed that Seale had several body guards standing immediately behind him while Seale was talking with informant and others in informant's group behind the podium. All of these bodyguards were carrying guns and their actions were disciplined such as that used in the military.

Informant was present for the last part of Seale's public speech when he spoke of the Black Panther factories which produce food and clothing and the Black Panther farms. Seale also made the following public statement: 'You FBI m... f..., we know you're here.'

While behind the podium, informant also personally met John Lennon (former member of the Beatles band). Lennon spoke in definite anti-law enforcement tones and is a strong believer in the movement and the overthrow of the present society in America today.

Informant advised that Stevie Wonder was present, that he entertained and made a plea for peace. Informant also saw Reverend Dennis Moloney, Reverend James Blakeslie (associate of Moloney) and John Sinclair's wife (who appeared to be 'stoned').

AIRTEL

TO: DIRECTOR, FBI

FROM: SAC, DETROIT (100-40422) (C)

FREEDOM RALLY, UNIVERSITY OF MICHIGAN,
ANN ARBOR, MICHIGAN, 12/10/71,
SPONSORED BY COMMITTEE TO FREE
JOHN SINCLAIR

DO NOT DESTROY ~~~~ 20

PRIOR TO ~~~~

SM - NEW LEFT; TRAVEL OF DEFENDENTS;
IS - WHITE PANTHER PARTY

FOIPA

Re Detroit teletype to Bureau, 12/11/71.

Enclosed for the Bureau are five (5) copies of
a LHM setting forth information regarding captioned rally.
Copies of LHM being furnished to below-listed offices for
information purposes: (U)

LHM classified confidential to protect the identity
of sources utilized therein whose identities if disclosed
could be detrimental to the national defense interests
of this nation. (U)

Sources identified as follows:

Source one is [redacted] (U)
Source two is Intelligence Unit, Mich. State
    Police (U)

2 - Bureau (Enc. 5) (RM)
2 - Boston (Enc. 2) (RM)
2 - Chicago (Enc.2)(RM)
    (1 - 176-5) (1 - 157-3315)(RM)
2 - Milwaukee (157-1785) (Enc. 2)(RM)
2 - New York (100-174910) (Enc. 2) (RM)
2 - San Francisco (176-2) (Enc. 2) (RM)
2 - WFO (1 - 100-[redacted] (Enc. 2) (RM)
    (1 - NATIONAL STUDENT ASSOCIATION)
5 - Detroit (2 - 100-40422) (1 - 100-40452)
    (1 - 176-219) (1 - 176-68)
JBR:js
(19)   9-22-78

DO NOT DESTROY
PENDING LITIGATION

December 27, 1971

Re: Freedom Rally, University of Michigan, Ann Arbor,
      Michigan, December 10, 1971, sponsored by Committee to
      Free John Sinclair

Alan Ginsberg is a New York based poet and philosopher. Jane Kennedy is reportedly a Women's Liberation representative. Tabankin is the President of the National Student Association, Washington, DC.

Source two advised December 3, 1971, that the WPP has in the past made intense efforts to legalize marijuana and that Sinclair has become the symbol of that effort.

On December 8, 1971, source one advised that during a second press conference by David Sinclair, Lennie Sinclair and David Fenton, all officers of WPP, Ann Arbor, it was announced that the following additional persons were scheduled to speak at the December 10, 1971, Free John Sinclair Rally: Fr James Groppi, Robert Williams, former head, Republic of New Africa, a Black militant organization, and John Lennon and his wife, Yoko Ono.

Source advised further that several national and international rock bands were scheduled for above rally.

Source advised that attendance cost to the rally was set at $3.00 per person. Source advised that because of an anticipated over-flow of persons at the rally hall, which hall seats 15,000 persons, the following allocation of tickets was made: 6,000 – Ann Arbor, Michigan; 4,000 – Detroit, Michigan; 1,000 each Jackson, Flint, Lansing, Saginaw and Grand Rapids, Michigan.

Source four advised December 11, 1971, that the rally began at 7.15 p.m., December 10, 1971, at the University of Michigan

Events Building, Ann Arbor. Source advised the rally terminated at approximately 3.30 a.m., December 11, 1971, with estimated attendance of 15,000 to 16,000 persons.

Source five advised December 13, 1971, rally was attended by an estimated 15,000 persons and terminated in the early morning hours of December 11, 1971, without any incidents. Source advised 10 off-duty Ann Arbor police officers patroled the area near the rally hall. Source advised the services of the off-duty police officers were obtained and paid for at a cost of $150.00 by the WPP at Ann Arbor, Michigan. Source advised police officers patroled only on the outside of the rally hall and were not permitted to enter rally.

Source advised the entire portion of the rally hall was patroled by so-called WPP Rangers, also known as The Psychedelic Rangers.

Source six advised December 13, 1971, University of Michigan facilities for captioned rally were obtained by unknown persons on or about November 30, 1971, at a cost of $4,000.00, which was paid for in cash and in advance. Source advised approximately five well-known rock bands and/or singers performed at the rally, including John Lennon and wife Yoko Ono. Lennon formerly with group known as the Beatles. Source advised Lennon prior to rally composed the following song entitled, 'John Sinclair', which song Lennon sang at the rally. Source advised this song was composed by Lennon especially for this event.

On December 13, 1971, source six advised he learned from Lennie Sinclair, officer WPP, that the Detroit Committee to Free John Sinclair netted a total of $26,000.00 from the rally.

Following are verbatim speeches of William Kunstler, Rennie Davis, Jerry Rubin and others as indicated:

BOB RUDNICK – MC

People have come from various parts of the planet to help get

John out. All right, Bobby Seale will be here, Phil Oaks, Jerry Rubin, Sheila Murphy, the UP, Ed Sanders, Commander Codi, Rennie Davis, Lennie Sinclair, Archie Shepp (phonetic), Father Groppi, a special guest, and then David Peel with John Lennon and Yoko Ono.

The lost-and-found and drug help is in the north-west, I think that's over there, if you need it. Right now we're gonna have a tape. Ok, this is gonna be an all-night long hassle, we gotta keep the aisles clear, the fireman are running around so if possible we're gonna have to keep announcing, just keep the lanes as clear as you can.

William Kunstler is a little busy with a new case. He's trying to get someone else out of jail and couldn't be here, so to send a message he put it on tape and we're gonna have that in about 10 seconds.

WILLIAM KUNSTLER (TAPED MESSAGE)

I have tried everything I could to be in Ann Arbor tonight but it is impossible. But I know that so many of John Sinclair's friends will be with you that my absence will be more keenly felt by me than by anyone else. Yet I could not let the night go by without at least making this tape, unsatisfactory as it is, to give some concrete form to my devotion to John and the cause which he symbolizes and represents.

John is in jail for two essential reasons: first of all he is a political person who calls into question the validity of the super state which seeks to control all of us and destroys those it cannot readily dominate. Secondly, his harsh sentence dramatizes the absurdity of our marijuana laws, which are irrational, unjust and indefensible. Recently, the National Institute of Mental Health submitted to the Congress its 176-page report 'Marijuana and Health', which comes to the conclusion that 'for the bulk of smokers, marijuana does not seem to be harmful'. Yet it is made a crime in every state with penalties ranging in severity from life to six months in jail. On the other hand, conventional cigarettes can be legally sold as long as they bear a legend on the package that they can cause serious illness or death.

We will have 20 in the next 8 months and we might have 30 in the next two years. At the same time we are going to have a quantitative increase in every major oppressed community in the country. Got to happen! It's the only way we are going to attack capitalism – to expropriate from that capitalist system the goods, the technology, etc., put it down in the poor oppressed communities – all of us the people that are oppressed and us too – and everybody processing it and giving it away free. It's the only way I know to start attacking the monster of capitalism. A monster of charging people money for everything they get, we're saying the music is free, the life is free, the world is free and if it ain't free, let's start getting our chains off now – the psychology chains and the chains of oppression. Let's get it off now. Let's have the chains off of us now, because if we don't have the chains off of us they are going to annihilate us. They are going to annihilate us by polluting this earth – the capitalists and the fascists they are going to do this here. We're saying the universe belongs to the people. Mars belongs to the people and the people belong to the people – all power to the people. Thank you very much. Right on, power to the people.

JERRY RUBIN
… Also, Pun Plamondon is in jail; he is also with the Rainbow Peoples Party. He was the first person to become a fugitive and go underground in this country, and then he was caught and now he's in jail and we ought to have this rally to free Pun Plamondon and to free the 2,000 people who are now in jail for smoking dope, most of whom are black, and you see what people are going to

feel most across the country, when they hear about this rally. Think of all the prisoners behind bars, how they are going to feel, fed shit food, isolated, treated like animals and if they do anything courageous they lose their good time, and they have to stay in jail longer and longer. This rally is going to be the first prison rally all across the country demanding that they lay down the bars and let all the prisoners out. And while letting all the prisoners out, they ought to jail the judges, because every judge, every judge, should spend six months in a jail to see what it's like. To see what the feeling is of being locked up, and see whether that makes you feel any more human.

This is the first event of the Rock Liberation Front, and it's really incredible that John Lennon and Yoko Ono are going to be here tonight, and we should really think of what the meaning of that is. Because it's really a committed act by people who are very involved in music, who are identifying to the culture you and I are part of, the family that you and I are part of. And for them to come on this stage, and for John to sing a song 'It ain't fair, John Sinclair' and for John and Yoko to sing a song about the IRA and Attica state – it's really incredible. It shows that right now we can really unite music and revolutionary politics and really build the movement all across the country. [Applause] It's like a whole, it's like a whole cultural renaissance is about to begin and if John and Yoko can come here, we really have to go back to high school and colleges and communities and rebuild the movement to rebuild the revolution, because all the people who say the movement and the revolution is over should see what's going on right here, because it doesn't look over to me.

But there are there are a lot of problems, for example the amount of heroin and dope that is smoked in the black and white youth communities is really serious – so many young, 15, 16, 17-year-old kids who are totally wiped out on downers because they

John Sinclair reunited with his daughters on his release on bond after serving 28 months of his 9^1/$_2$–10 year sentence for marijuana possession (December 1971)

have to find some way to get through the prison of high school and college and some way out of the prison of America, instead of building a revolutionary movement. The amount of heroin that is floating around our communities, we have to drive the heroin pushers out of our communities and build [applause]. So heroin is poison and you know it gets its source from south-east Asia --- and then it's shipped by the CIA back to the US as a poison to poison us so we don't make a revolution – that's why they are pushing all this heroin into us. [Applause]

Also, there is like a very strange spirit among young people today, a spirit of tremendous mistrust, a spirit of which anybody who takes an action, calls a demonstration, comes forward with something, is attacked by someone else in the movement for being an ego-tripper or media freak or doing something wrong. It's a total anti-leadership spirit, so the people are afraid to take the initiative or afraid to take actions, not because of what the pig might do, but afraid to take action because of what their own brothers and sisters might say about them.

It's a very strange thing that people are afraid to speak out, and that's why there's such a quiet across the country – because the moment somebody does something, someone else right next to him says, 'I didn't like what you did'.

We have to give each other a chance to make mistakes, we have to give each other a chance [inaudible] because if we are our own worst critics, no one is going to do anything, we are going to be paralyzed in fear and all the violence and hostilities that we felt against.

And John Sinclair is a key person in the liberation struggle, in the struggle to liberate all the people from the overt and the covert prisons, from the prisons behind bars and outside bars, and we need John Sinclair out of prison not only for his own sake but to help in that struggle. John Sinclair has united rock and revolu-

Washington, DC, April 1971: During the Veterans Against the War in Vietnam demonstrations

tion. He has united a position to political repression and to economic exploitation. He's united opposition from domestic oppression and foreign aggression, and we want John Sinclair out of prison.

We want him out of prison to help us organize the music at San Diego. [Applause] And we want him out of prison to organize the music in a lot of events like this one that will take place up and down the country between now and San Diego to get those other prisoners out of jail – out of the jail of the factories that they are in, out of the jail of the money system, out of the jail of the foreign policy.

Now I'm just going to say one sentence about the war, and I think Rennie indicated already that Nixon's program is not for winding down the war but for winding down the anti-war movement. It's the most cynical appeal to us, to say it doesn't matter that more people are being killed today than there were last month; it doesn't matter that there were more people killed last month than there were under Johnson, as long as they are Asians, as long as they are not Americans but [if] you want a real clue to that kind of cynicism, I'll quote one of my political advisers, George Wallace.

George Wallace came up with a shadow cabinet yesterday and who do you suppose his secretary of state was? Ambassador William Porter, who is Nixon's ambassador to the Vietnamese peace talks. That tells you what's happening to the Vietnamese peace talks. That tells you what's happening to the war under the Nixon program.

Now one last point: I also came here tonight to hear John and Yoko, and so did a lot of other people, but I came here to hear John and Yoko sing a song to the liberation of John Sinclair and the other prisoners.

We have the power, we have the strength – if, like the

Vietnamese and the Cambodians and the Laotians, we do not allow the Government, visible or invisible, to pacify us, if we do not allow them to convince them that we are weak and impotent and that nothing we do will matter.

Ever since 1964, the press, the dove press mind you, and the Government has been saying that the war is ending and the anti-war movement is dead, but it has never been through, and it is not through today, the war will not go away by itself, and John Sinclair will not get free by …

LETTER TO THE EDITOR
The Village Voice, December 30, 1971

A.J. COME, A.J. GO

To John, Yoko, Jerry and David – you come to America, check out of the St Regis Hotel, and check into the Village, where you immediately strike up a friendship with Jerry Rubin, who is into everything you want to get into.

Jerry, after all being a Yippie with Yippie tendencies, introduces you to David Peel, the 'park bench singer', who just happens to be without a recording contract. Zam. David Peel breaks into Apple Records.

Now David, as far back as we can remember, you and Weberman were a duet. Remember 'A.J. A.J. Weberman'? No, I guess not. I mean, when it comes to choosing between being famous or having a real friend, being famous will always win out.

John Lennon, being 'the' John Lennon, met Bob Dylan and naturally they began rapping. Between the rap, Dylan must have mentioned that a guy named Alan Julius Weberman had been bothering him for the longest time. Lennon later, upon seeing Rubin and Peel, mentioned that Dylan had told him Weberman was a pest and he (Dylan) didn't know how to get rid of him. Lennon, Rubin and Peel immediately took it upon themselves to help Dylan get rid of Weberman. Rubin called A.J. up, and who knows what they said to him. Weberman immediately wrote an apology into *The Voice* (December 9) who promptly misquoted him on one word which changed the context of the whole letter.

The question here is, exactly what was used to convince A.J. to mend his ways. Was it Lennon's money? Or was it Rubin's threat?

Name withheld
Manhattan Beach

1972

UNITED STATES GOVERNMENT

Memorandum

~~SECRET~~

TO : S-7C, New York (100-157178)

DATE: 1/12/72

FROM : SA ████████████████ b7c

SUBJECT: Jerry Clyde Rubin, AKA
SM-YIP (EXTREMIST)
(Key Activist)

The subject appeared with John Lennon and Yoko Ono at a press conference taped and shown on WABC-TV "Eyewitness News" at 6:00 pm on 1/11/72. The press conference was held in NYC and only Lennon was interviewed.

Rubin appeared to have his hair cut much shorter than previously shown in other photographs.

ALL EXTREMISTS SHOULD BE CONSIDERED DANGEROUS.

CLASS. & EXT. BY ████ 4/19/82
REASON-FCIM II, 1-2, 4.2 (2), (3)
DATE OF REVIEW ████████ 110157178.

SEARCHED _____ INDEXED _____
SERIALIZED ████ FILED _____
42 JAN ██
FBI — NEW YORK

b7c

1703

1-100-157178 (47)

SAC NEW YORK TO DIRECTOR AND SACs, NEWARK, SAN DIEGO, WASHINGTON FIELD

January 21, 1972
Subject: Allamuchy Tribe
Security matter: IS – New Left, CALREP

Instant date, source, who has furnished reliable information in the past, advised that the Allamuchy Tribe is to open an office in NYC during the next two weeks. Source states this group was formed from meetings held at the Peter Stuyvesant Farm, Allamuchy, NJ, during the last month. Members of this group, headed by Rennie Davis, include Stu Albert, J. Craven. Source noted all individuals participating in this entity were hard-core New Left activists formerly associated with Mayday and People's Coalition for Peace and Justice (PCPJ). Source further advised the purpose of this group was to direct movement activities during the election year to culminate with demonstrations at the Republican convention August next. Source noted a large sum of money has been given to this group by John Lennon. John Lennon is identified as former member of the Beatles rock group, who is currently residing in NYC.

ADMINISTRATIVE
Source is identified as ***. The New York office is opening a separate case captioned 'Allamuchy Tribe'. Copy provided San Diego due to interest in forthcoming national convention. Information copy provided Newark.

Washington Field: Contact sources re activities of Rennie Davis and PCPJ. Forward any information re formation Allamuchy Tribe.

John Lennon flashing a peace sign as he and Yoko Ono arrive at the New York office of Immigration and Naturalization Service to fight deportation proceedings, May 1972

TELETYPE
NEW YORK TO DIRECTOR FBI AND SACs NEWARK, SAN DIEGO, WASHINGTON FIELD

January 24, 1972
Subject: Allamuchy Tribe
Security matter: New Left, CALREP

Instant date, source who has furnished reliable information in the past advised as follows:

Captioned group has rented two stories of warehouse spaces on Hudson Street to be used as offices. This space presently being equipped with furnishings and office equipment and will be operational near future. Allegedly John Lennon has contributed $75,000 and one, ***, $15,000 to aid in the formation of captioned entity.

Rennie Davis purported one of the initial aims of this group would be to attempt to purchase the *Liberation News Service*. Due to the LNS financial crisis Davis plans to use LNS as a media tool of the Allamuchy Tribe.

ADMINISTRATIVE
Re NY teletype, January 21, last. Source is identified as ***. ***. NYO is affording close coverage of matter on advice of Bureau.

MOMENTS OF HISTORY |

62

2/13/96

CLASSIFIED BY: SSA 9803 R00/JS CONFIDENTIAL 1724/72
REASON: 1.5 (C)
DECLASSIFY ON: X /
CA# CV83-1720
TELETYPE SPACH/NLT   CODE

9/25/97
CLASSIFIED BY SSA 56686 LD/S
DECLASSIFY ON: 25X1
CA# 83-1720

CLASSIFIED DECISIONS FINALIZED
BY DEPARTMENT REVIEW COMMITTEE (DRC)
DATE: 12/10/97
CA# 83-1720
SSA 510/JS 12/10/97

URGENT

TO   : DIRECTOR, FBI (ATT: DID) AND SACS, NEWARK, SAN DIEGO
            WASHINGTON FIELD

FROM   : NEW YORK (100-New)

SUBJECT : ALLAMUCHY TRIBE
            IS-NEW LEFT
            CALREP

CA# 83-1720
9803 R00/JS 7/2/92
CLASS. BY SP/ SSK/RRB
1-13-83

INSTANT DATE SOURCE WHO HAS FURNISHED RELIABLE

INFORMATION IN THE PAST ADVISED AS FOLLOWS: (X)(U)

CAPTIONED GROUP HAS RENTED TWO STORIES OF WAREHOUSE

SPACE ON HUDSON ST. TO BE USED AS OFFICES. THIS SPACE PRESENTLY

BEING EQUIPPED WITH FURNISHINGS AND OFFICE EQUIPMENT AND WILL

BE OPERATIONAL NEAR FUTURE. ALLEGEDLY JOHN LENNON HAS

CONTRIBUTED SEVENTY FIVE THOUSAND DOLLARS AND ONE, ██████ b7C

FIFTEEN THOUSAND DOLLARS TO AID IN THE FORMATION OF CAPTIONED (X)(U)

ENTITY.

100-175319 2/72

1- New York ██████
1- New York ██████
1- New York (100-163426)(RENNIE DAVIS)
1- New York (100-   ) (JOHN LENNON)
1- New York (100-   ) ██████
1- New York (100-163260) (LMS) b7C
1- New York
1- Supv. #42
1- Supv. #47

RTR:FAR Raw
(9)

6-14-42   8369/She/alm/mg

CLASS. & EXT BY
REASON-FCIM II, 1.2.4.2

100-175319-4

SEARCHED
SERIALIZED
FILED OK
JAN 3

SAC NEW YORK TO DIRECTOR FBI AND SACs NEWARK, PITTSBURGH, PHILADELPHIA, SAN DIEGO, WASHINGTON FIELD

January 28, 1972

Subject: Changed, Election Year Strategy Information Center (EYSIC)

Security matter: New Left, CALREP

Title 'Changed' due to group being organized by Rennie Davis, formerly known as Allamuchy Tribe, has now changed its name as the public will soon become aware of its existence and purpose (anti-CALREP activities).

First source, who has furnished reliable information in the past, advised this date EYSIC has moved into office space in the vicinity of Tenth Street and Hudson Street, etc. EYSIC was formed for purpose of directing New Left activities during election year to culminate with demonstrations at the Republican convention August, next.

A second source, who has furnished reliable information in the past, advised January 27, last, members of group include Jerry Rubin, Stu Albert, Rennie Davis, Jay Craven, Carol Cullen, Carol Katchen and [Mike] Drobenare. Major financial backer appears to be John Lennon, formerly of the Beatles rock music group. Source advised Albert and Rubin are in constant contact with Lennon regarding group.

Second source advised January 21, last, that a faction of the People's Coalition for Peace and Justice (PCPJ) met at Allamuchy, New Jersey, on December 17, 1971, thru 18, 1971, and that they have since held a meeting at a farm located in Penn, exact place unknown. Group included before-mentioned individuals.

PCPJ self-described as organization consisting of over 100 organizations using massive civic disobedience to combat war, racism, poverty and repression. Its national office located at 156 Fifth Ave., NYC, room 527.

ADMINISTRATIVE
ReNYtel to Bureau, January, 21, last, captioned 'Allamuchy Tribe, IS – New Left, CALREP'.

First source is *** second source is ***.

Copy of tel being sent Pittsburgh and Philadelphia for future lead value.

New York attempting to locate office space EYSIC so as to effect appropriate coverage.

Newark at Allamuchy, New Jersey: Identify existence of Peter Stuyvesant farm and occupants.

Two: Immediately obtain toll calls for name at farm for past three months. Submit to New York and Bureau, attn: ADP Unit – New Left section.

Three: Survey sources.

Washington Field: Contact sources regarding activities your subjects Davis and Cullen concerning this group. Sutel results of above leads.

SAC NEW YORK TO DIRECTOR FBI AND SAC WASHINGTON FIELD

February 2, 1972

Subject: Election Year Strategy Information Center (EYSIC)

Security matter: New Left (CALREP)

On instant date personnel at INS, NYC, advised that John Winston Lennon, date of birth October 9, 1940, place of birth England, arrived NYC on August 11, 1968, under a B–2 visitor's status. He left the United States and re-entered, now holding a H–1 temporary visa status which expires end of February instant. Lennon has applied for another B–2 status leading up to becoming a United States citizen. INS file located central office INS, WDC, charged to basis Mason telephone 202–626–1336. Lennon's alien number A17597321.

He is presently married to Yoko Ono Lennon. ★★★

INS list NYC residence as Saint Regis Hotel, 150 Bank Street. Lennon has since moved to unknown address.

LEAD
Washington Field Office immediately review INS file regarding Lennon, and forward background including photo of subject to NYO.

Jerry Rubin and Abbie Hoffman, two of the seven charged with conspiring to incite the riots which tore Chicago during the 1968 Democratic Convention, facing newsmen during a recess in the 1970 trial. All convictions in this trial were overturned on appeal.

TO: SAC, BOSTON
FROM: SAC, NEW YORK (100-169939)
SUBJECT: PCPJ
SM-NEW LEFT

Date prepared

Date received	Received from (name or symbol number)	Received by
2/2/72	▓▓▓▓ b2 b7D	▓▓▓▓ b7C

Method of delivery (check appropriate blocks)

[X] in person [ ] by telephone [ ] by mail [ ] orally [ ] recording device [X] written by Informa

If orally furnished and reduced to writing by Agent: Date	Date of Report
Dictated _____ to _____	2/1/72
	Date(s) of activity
Transcribed _____	
Authenticated by Informant _____	2/1/72

Brief description of activity or material

PCPJ Activity

File where original is located if not attache
▓▓▓▓ b2 b7D

* INDIVIDUALS DESIGNATED BY AN ASTERISK (*) ONLY ATTENDED A MEETING AND DID NOT ACTIVELY PARTICIPAT
VIOLENCE OR REVOLUTIONARY ACTIVITIES WERE NOT DISCUSSED.

[ ] Information recorded on a card index by _____ on date _____

Remarks:

DECLASSIFIED ON 5-2-83
BY 1678 REP/EAn

All necessary action taken.

1 - Boston (NHPCPJ) (RM)
1 - Washington Field Office (100-   ) (R. DAVIS) (RM)
1 - New York ▓▓▓▓▓▓ b2,b7D
1 - New York ▓▓▓▓▓▓ (42)
1 - New York ▓▓▓▓▓▓ (45) b7C
1 - New York ▓▓▓▓▓▓ (45)
1 - New York (100-157178) (J. RUBIN) (42)
1 - New York (100-172771) (MDC) (42)
1 - New York (100-21672) (D. DELLINGER) (42)
1 - New York (100-175319) (J. LENNON) (42)
1 - New York

▓▓▓▓ b7C

(12)

100 175319 26
Block Stamp

CLASS. & EXT. BY ▓▓▓▓
REASON FOR ▓▓▓▓ I 1 2 A 8
DATE OF REVIEW 8 ▓▓▓▓

ALL INFOR▓▓▓▓

SEARCHED _____	INDEXED _____
SERIALIZED _____	FILED _____

INFORMANT REPORT OF FEBRUARY I, 1972
SAC New York to SAC Boston

Received February 2, 1972
Subject: PCPJ activity
Security matter: New Left

***

Rennie Davis is staying at Jerry Rubin's house. May Day [Collective] is at odds with PCPJ.

Dave Dellinger is still in a hospital in Boston. Some people in Harrisburg committee said last Friday some Government agents were around. Please find some 3" x 5" cards of key contacts in the south-west. PCPJ is conducting a campaign of Pledge signing. The Pledge states that the signee will not support a war candidate. May Day promises that San Diego will be like Washington, but with 100 times the people.

Davis and Rubin still run May Day, but do not wish the public eye to be cast upon them so they are running the party from the background.

John Lennon is working very closely within May Day and there may be a peace concert next month in the Boston Garden. PCPJ refuses to pay any taxes, including the phone excise tax.

Barbara Webster will most likely be in the office Thursday (wait for my call).

INFORMANT REPORT OF FEBRUARY 6, 1972

Received February 14, 1972
Prepared March 8, 1972
Subject: Irish Republican Club Meeting, NYC, February 6, 1972

A meeting of the committee against internment in Northern Ireland took place at the Irish Institute at 326 West 48th St, at 4.05 p.m.

An amendment to the purpose of the group was made, so that the body was now not just against internment, but also for the immediate withdrawal of British troops from Northern Ireland.

A speaker from the floor asked that the purpose of the body be amended to include support for the Irish Republican Army in money and even in guns. This motion wasn't even accepted by the chair, and the gentleman declared he would leave the meeting.

A steering committee was set up after much discussion and argumentation. The original committee contained two representatives from the following clubs: Irish Republican Clubs, Northern Aid Committee, National Association for Irish Freedom and the American Committee for Ulster Justice.

Members of the Socialist Workers Party were present, and they came into the meeting as a unit and argued the following points: 'with four organizations it's packed (the steering committee) … the steering committee must be broad, the four organizations have shown that they can't cooperate freely … it is important that the steering committee be representative of all tendencies and individuals … those people who want to take responsibility will be able to do so (in the broad steering committee). There are talented people who want to do work.'

The broad steering committee motion was passed.

A March 1st or 4th action date was proposed. The SWP people

called for a mass demonstration.

It was announced that John Lennon had offered entertainment. One route proposed was a march from Columbus Circle to Bryant Park, or Central Park.

Someone suggested that all British people, and all British organizations, be harassed, as the Jewish Defense League does with the Soviets.

A boycott of British goods was proposed.

It was suggested that the Irish ask the Chinese in the Hotel Roosevelt (Red Chinese) to talk to Nixon when he is in Peking. This idea was strongly put down.

Three members of the SWP (if not more) were named to the steering committee: Ray 'Marky' (1930-local of the New York Public Library System), Gene 'Bertine' of Local 1199, and Nat London, formerly of the Peace Action Coalition. In all 28 names were accepted for the committee.

The Irish Republican Clubs are aware of the presence of SWP people, and they are watching them. Mary Cotter was a spokesman for the Irish group, and she's a SWP person (this occurred at a BOAC demonstration previous to this meeting), and as such served the interests of the Irish group rather than the SWP.

SAC NEW YORK TO DIRECTOR FBI

February 17, 1972
Subject: Youth Election Strategy, aka Project 'YES'
Security matter: IS – New Left

ReBuairtel February 15, 1972.

On February 17, 1972, *** advised that the Youth Election Strategy is the videotape arm of the Election Year Strategy Information Center, which will eventually attempt to purchase the *Liberation News Service* in New York City. This group is controlled by John Lennon, Rennie Davis and Jerry Rubin, who are also the key figures in EYSIC. They will make the contacts for videotapes, films, special events and entertainers to raise money for the group to finance EYSIC's anti-CALREP demonstrations.

At the present they have no separate office in New York City; however, they are working out of the Global Village, which is a media-TV type of organization.

DECLASSIFY ON: 25X 6

CA# 83-1720

~~SECRET~~

In Reply, Please Refer to
File No.

CLASSIFIED BY: 9803RDD ~~CONFIDENTIAL~~

REASON: 1.5 (b)

DECLASSIFY ON: X 5

CA # eV 83-1720

February 22, 1972

CLASSIFIED DECISIONS FINALIZE
BY DEPARTMENT REVIEW COMM
DATE 12/10/97

JOHN WINSTON LENNON

b7D

X(5)

b7D   stated that

X(6)

CLASS. & EXT. BY
REASON FCIM II
DATE OF REVIEW

SEARCHED ___ INDEXED ___
SERIALIZED ___ FILED ___
MAR 3 1972
FBI—NEW YORK

GROUP 2
Excluded from automatic
downgrading and

UNITED STATES DEPARTMENT OF JUSTICE – FBI, WASHINGTON, DC

February 22, 1972
Subject: John Winston Lennon

*** ***

*** advised on February 15, 1972, that John Winston Lennon, born October 9, 1940, in Liverpool, England, on November 28, 1968, at Marylebone Magistrates Court, London, pleaded guilty to possessing dangerous drugs (cannabis). He was fined £150 and ordered to pay £21 costs.

The records of the Visa Section, American Embassy, London, of February 15, 1972, revealed that John Lennon last appeared at this Embassy on August 13, 1971. He was issued a B–1 and B–2 (business and pleasure) visa for one entry to the United States for a six-week period, after a waiver of his visa ineligibility because of his criminal conviction had been cleared with US Immigration and Naturalization Service.

UNITED STATES DEPARTMENT OF JUSTICE – FBI, NEW YORK

February 25, 1972
Subject: Jerry Clyde Rubin

On February 22, 1972, Jerry Rubin appeared on the Mike Douglas television show which was aired on Channel II, Columbia Broadcasting System, from 4.30 p.m. to 6.00 p.m. John Lennon, formerly with the Beatles musical group, and his wife were co-hosts on this show. This program was tape recorded and pertinent statements made by Rubin are included in this memorandum.

Mike Douglas introduced Jerry Rubin, stating his feelings were quite negative concerning Rubin but that John Lennon wanted him on the show.

John Lennon stated that Rubin was not at all like his image as he and his wife were not like their image. He stated he found something in Rubin that was artistic.

Mike Douglas asked: 'What is Jerry Rubin thinking about these days?'

Rubin stated: 'Glad you asked that! We're going to support Nixon for president, because by going to China he is furthering communist revolution throughout the world, and also encouraging communism at home. Anything to get elected! Even though it's not appreciated by the right wing, it's appreciated by the left – I'm just kidding! What he has really done is automate the war in Vietnam so that its machines killing people create a situation where 43 people can be murdered at Attica, create a situation where four kids can be killed at Kent State and people are afraid. The atmosphere of the country is one of his debts. I think the Administration did this, and he is the symbol of it. And so I'm working very hard with people all over the country to defeat Nixon.'

Kent, Ohio, May 1970: Hundreds of university students staged a demonstration in protest against the Nixon administration's expansion of the Vietnam war into Cambodia. When the tear gas fired by the masked national guardsmen dissipated, four students lay dead and several others were injured.

When questioned about the 'Movement', Rubin stated that 'the way the movement has changed is the pressure is so heavy that if anybody does anything, gets arrested, jailed, killed, that people are very pessimistic.'

Douglas stated he had heard that Rubin was against drugs and this was the reason he was in favor of having him on the program. Rubin stated he was not against drugs but against heroin. Rubin stated: 'The police are the protectors of the heroin trade, and heroin is used against black people and against some white people right now, as a killer drug. Too many young kids are taking downers and heroin, because they see no future for themselves in this country, they see no hope in changing the country, they see no decent life in which they can be creative and express themselves, so they shoot into their veins and take a pill. And that's the society's fault, as it offers no alternative. As a revolutionary movement, we've got to give an alternative.'

When questioned about voting, Rubin stated that all young people should vote as a block, just like women should vote as a block. 'We've got to get Nixon out of the White House because we've got to stop the automated war in Vietnam. It's power if we vote together. We shouldn't vote for any candidate that doesn't automatically withdraw everything from Vietnam. And we ought to go to both conventions in Miami and San Diego and non-violently make our presence felt – and stand on the issues. If we do anything any other way, we'll be killed.'

When questioned as to what he thinks is right in this country, Rubin stated that what's right is the fact that there are people in the country who want to change it. He stated that what he thought was beautiful about it is that the children of America want to change the country and are going to.

UNITED STATES DEPARTMENT OF JUSTICE – FBI
San Diego, California

February 25, 1972
Subject: Youth Election Strategy, also known as Project 'YES'

On February 3, 1972, a confidential source advised that a group headed by Rennard Cordon Davis also known as Rennie Davis, is in its first phase of planning for disruption at the Republican National Convention (RNC) to be held in San Diego, California, from August 21–August 23, 1972. According to this source Davis and other associates from the People's Coalition for Peace and Justice (PCPJ) recently moved from Washington, DC, to New York City.

> Rennard Cordon Davis is a convicted defendant of the so-called Conspiracy 7 Trial, Chicago, Illinois, in the period September, 1969–February, 1970, involving those persons earlier indicted for violation of the Federal Anti-Riot Statute.

> PCPJ in a press release dated March 1, 1971, described itself as being headquartered in Washington, DC, and consisting of over 100 organizations which are using massive civil disobedience to combat racism, poverty, repression and war.

According to this source, the plans for San Diego include rock concerts featuring John Lennon, formerly of the Beatles rock music group, and his wife, Yoko Ono, as the main crowd-drawers backed up by lesser rock group talents.

It was further related by this source that dates have reportedly been arranged in Florida and New Hampshire, and the concerts will include speeches by Jerry Rubin and Rennie Davis, along with Lennon, who will urge the audience to (a) register to vote; (b) work for the legalization of marijuana; and (c) get to San Diego for the GOP Convention.

This source further stated that conflicting reports make it difficult to analyze the proposed activities of John Lennon at this time. While this source indicates Lennon may be coming to San Diego, other indications are that he will perform along the East Coast only and contribute a portion of his proceeds to the San Diego Convention Coalition (SDCC).

> Jerry Rubin is a convicted defendant of the so-called Conspiracy 7 Trial, Chicago, Illinois, in the period of September, 1969–February, 1970, involving those persons earlier indicted for violation of the Federal Anti-Riot Statute.

> SDCC is a group comprised of representatives of various radical groups in San Diego, California, which was formed for active opposition to the United States Government through 'serious, determined, and long-term social upheaval'.

The aforementioned confidential source, along with other confidential sources familiar with certain phases of New Left activity in the San Diego area, advised on February 24, 1972, that information has been received in San Diego regarding proposed activities of a group headed by Rennie Davis and including John Lennon in connection with the RNC, but no specific information has been received regarding any such activities under the name of Election Year Strategy Information Center (EYSIC) or Youth Election

Strategy, also known as Project 'YES'.

> EYSIC is a group formed from meetings held at the Peter
> Stuyvesant Farm, Allamuchy, New Jersey, during December,
> 1971. The group is headed by Rennie Davis and was organ-
> ized for the purpose of directing New Left activities during
> the election year and to culminate with demonstrations at
> the 1972 RNC. On January 28, 1972, the group changed its
> name from Allamuchy Tribe to EYSIC.

> Youth Election Strategy, also known as Project 'YES', is the
> video-tape arm of EYSIC which will eventually attempt to
> purchase the *Liberation News Service* in New York City. This
> group is controlled by John Lennon, Rennie Davis and Jerry
> Rubin, who are also key figures in EYSIC. They will make the
> contacts for video tapes, films, special events and entertainers
> to raise money for the group to finance demonstrations
> in opposition to the RNC.

Liberation News Service (LNS) publishes news packets in New York
City on a weekly basis and the packets are sold to radical New Left
underground newspapers.

SAC NEW YORK TO DIRECTOR FBI

March 2, 1972

Subject: Election Year Strategy Information Center

Security matter: IS – New Left (CALREP)

Re NY airtel and LHM dated February 28, 1972; and San Diego airtel and LHM dated February 25, 1972, captioned 'Youth Election Strategy IS – NL'.

On March 2, 1972, ***, Immigration Officer, Immigration and Naturalization Service, 20 West Broadway, NYC, advised that on March 1, 1972, INS served notice to John Winston Lennon and his wife Yoko Ono Lennon to be out of the United States by March 15, 1972, that their visas had been recalled.

LEAD

At New York, New York: Will keep Bureau advised.

MEMORANDUM – UNITED STATES GOVERNMENT
SUPERVISOR *** #311 TO SAC NEW YORK

March 7, 1972
Subject: John Winston Lennon
Security matter: New Left

On March 7, 1972, INS Investigator *** telephonically advised that captioned and his wife, Yoko Ono, were served on March 6, 1972, with an order to show cause as to why they should not be deported from the US as over-stayed visitors.

Review of NY indices reflects ident case file as indicated presently assigned to Rotor #42.

The foregoing is furnished for information.

TELETYPE
FBI COMMUNICATIONS SECTION
NEW YORK TO DIRECTOR

March 16, 1972
Subject: John Winston Lennon
Security matter: New Left

On March 16, instant, Mr Vincent Schiano, chief trial attorney, INS, NYC, advised that John Lennon and his wife Yoko Ono appeared at INS, NYC, this date for deportation proceedings. Both individuals through their attorney won delay of hearings. Lennon requested delay while he attempted to fight a narcotics conviction in England. Yoko Ono requested delay on basis of child custody case in which she is involved.

Mr Schiano advised that new hearings would be held on April 18, next. If Lennon wins overthrow of British narcotic conviction, INS will reconsider their attempts to deport Lennon and wife. Schiano advised there was extensive news coverage at hearings both inside and out of building. Lennon spoke with local United Press International (UPI) and Associated Press (AP) representatives when he left hearings and claimed he was framed in British narcotics arrest.

NYO following.

DOMESTIC INTELLIGENCE DIVISION
Informative Note

March 17, 1972

You were previously advised that John Winston Lennon, and his wife, Yoko Ono, are in the US and that Lennon is the major financial contributor to Election Year Strategy Information Center (EYSIC) which was organized to conduct disruptive demonstrations during the Republican National Convention. EYSIC has been 'dying on the vine' recently due to Lennon's imminent deportation and recent dissatisfaction with Rennie Davis, militant revolutionary, who is the head of EYSIC.

Attached states that Lennon and his wife appeared at the Immigration and Naturalization Service (INS) in New York City on March 16, 1972, for deportation proceedings. Both Lennon and wife won delay until April 18, 1972; Lennon because he stated he was attempting to fight a narcotics conviction in England, the basis for his deportation; and Ono on the basis of a child custody case in which she is involved.

We are closely following these proceedings and you will be kept advised.

the following in _____
(Type in plaintext or code)

AIRTEL _____
(Priority)

TO: DIRECTOR, FBI (62-112678)

FROM: SAC, ALEXANDRIA (100-506) (P)

WHITE PANTHER PARTY (WPP)
IS-WPP
(OO: DETROIT)

CALREP   JOHN OLENNON

MIDEM

Re Detroit airtel to the Bureau dated 3/23/72, (no copy to Miami and San Diego); and Detroit letter to the Bureau, 3/15/72.

For the information of Miami and San Diego, referenced airtel contained information from Detroit that the White Panther Party (WPP) is not a structured organization in that WPP activities in several cities throughout the country are not contingent upon approval of the Detroit Chapter or otherwise.

cc 908) ' ????)

(4) - Bureau (By Courier)
2 - Chicago (RM)
2 - Detroit (100-36217) (RM)
2 - Miami (RM)
    (1 - 100-16553)
    (1 - 80-1353) (DEMCON)
2 - San Diego (RM)
    (1 - 80 - CALREP)
    (1 -   )
2 - Alexandria
    (1 - 100-506)
    (1 - 100-883) (CALREP)
RJI:1mm
(14)

62-112678

20 APR 3 1972

100-469910 -
NOT RECORDED
47 APR 13 1972

RESEARCH SECTION

oved: _____ APR 12 1972   Sent _____ M Per _____
58APR17 1972 Special Agent in Charge

U. S. GOVERNMENT PRINTING OFFICE: 1971-413-136

DIRECTOR FBI TO SAC NEW YORK

April 10, 1972
Subject: John Winston Lennon
Security matter: New Left

ReNYtel March 16, 1972.

Enclosed for information of New York are two copies of Alexandria airtel dated March 31, 1972, captioned 'White Panther Party, IS – WPP; CALREP; MIDEM', which contains information from Alexandria source relating to current activities of subject.

It appears from referenced New York teletype that subject and wife might be preparing for lengthy delaying tactics to avert their deportation in the near future. In the interim, very real possibility exists that subject, as indicated in enclosed airtel, might engage in activities in US leading toward disruption of Republican National Convention (RNC), San Diego, August 1972. For this reason New York promptly initiate discreet efforts to locate subject and remain aware of his activities and movements. Handle inquiries only through established sources and discreet pretext inquiries. Careful attention should be given to reports that subject is heavy narcotics user and any information developed in this regard should be furnished to narcotics authorities and immediately furnished to Bureau in form suitable for dissemination.

In view of subject's avowed intention to engage in disruptive activities surrounding RNC, New York Office will be responsible for closely following his activities until time of actual deportation. Afford this matter close supervision and keep Bureau fully advised by most expeditious means warranted.

Note:

John Lennon, former member of Beatles singing group, is allegedly in US to assist in organizing disruption of RNC. Due to narcotics conviction in England, he is being deported along with wife Yoko Ono. They appeared at Immigration and Naturalization Service, New York, March 16, 1972, for deportation proceedings but won delay until April 18, 1972, because subject fighting narcotics conviction and wife fighting custody child case in US. Strong possibility looms that subject will not be deported any time soon and will probably be in US at least until RNC. Information developed by Alexandria source that subject continues to plan activities directed toward RNC and will soon initiate series of 'rock concerts' to develop financial support, with first concert to be held Ann Arbor, Michigan, in near future. New York Office covering subject's temporary residence and being instructed to intensify discreet investigation of subject to determine activities vis-à-vis RNC.

On March 31, 1972, Alexandria source mentioned in referenced letter who has furnished reliable information in the past concerning the WPP and who has been characterized by the Detroit Office on the basis of information furnished as 'a competent observer and an efficient interviewer who obtained very factual and significant information' advised as follows:

> On March 26, 1972, *** told source that he had been recently contacted by one, ***, who is allegedly *** and who allegedly had some connection with the People's Coalition for Peace and Justice (PCJP) in 1968, and who was said to have taken part in planning Youth International Party (YIP) demonstrations at the Democratic National Convention in Chicago.
>
> *** told source that *** related to him that he had been in contact in the recent past with individuals who were

planning disruptive activities directed towards the
Republican National Convention in San Diego, California,
in August 1972.

    *** stated that there would be no organized effort to dis-
rupt the Democratic National Convention scheduled for
Miami, Florida, in July 1972, by this group as the Democrats
are currently destroying themselves and will need no assistance from anyone to disrupt their own convention.
However, 'there will be a lot of trouble at the Republic
National Convention in San Diego' and plans are currently
being discussed but not implemented as how to best achieve
this disruption. One of the primary reasons according to ***
as to why no active efforts have been made to implement
these plans is a lack of funds at the present time. This group
consists, according to ***, of people who were formerly
affiliated with the PCPJ and YIP, and who have some funds
left over from prior campaigns of these organizations.

    *** told *** that many former leaders of the PCPJ and
YIP have been discredited in the eyes of 'rank and file'
activists of these organizations as they feel that former leaders such as Jerry Rubin have 'become self-made superstars'
and are only interested in obtaining fame and publicity for
themselves rather than in the past stated goals of YIP and
other related groups.

Leadership of PCPJ and YIP, according to ***, is currently frag-
mented and the task of 'picking up the pieces' and putting
together an effective organization has been assumed by WPP
leader John Sinclair and a former member of the Beatles singing
group, John Lennon. Lennon and Sinclair are said to be working
together and devised the following plan to obtain funds to finance
activities against the Republican Convention:

Yoko Ono and John Lennon, c.1980

A series of 'rock concerts' featuring big-name established stars in the musical field as headliners and backed up with lesser known individuals and groups will be put on throughout the country. Lennon is said to have the know-how and the connections to achieve the above. These performances will provide the main source of funds needed by Lennon and Sinclair to carry out the disruptive tactics in San Diego. The first such concert, according to source, is to be held in the Chrysler Arena, Ann Arbor, Michigan, in the near future. This will be, according to ***, 'the opening gun of the campaign'.

Alexandria source again advised that *** reminded him that he desired no direct contact with the Federal Bureau of Investigation but would furnish information only to him. Additionally, for the information of the Bureau, Alexandria source still desires an interview with *** (Bureau refer to Alexandria airtel to Director, March 10, 1972).

Additionally, the above information if disseminated outside the Bureau could tend to compromise *** as it is not known how many individuals have had access to it.

LEADS
Chicago
At Chicago, Illinois: Will obtain background information on *** and advise Bureau and interested offices of any pertinent information.

Detroit
At Detroit, Michigan: 1. Will discreetly ascertain if a rock concert is scheduled to be held at the Chrysler Arena, Ann Arbor, in the near future.

2. Will attempt to obtain background information on *** and

advise Bureau and interested offices of pertinent information developed.

3. Will through established sources ascertain if Sinclair and Lennon are involved in attempt to cause disruption of the Republican Convention at San Diego, California, in August 1972.

4. Will advise Alexandria if any of the above information in the body of instant communication is verified in order to assist Alexandria in directing its source.

Alexandria

At Alexandria, Virginia: 1. Will submit LHM regarding the above information.

2. Will maintain contact with source and await results of investigation set forth above.

FEDERAL BUREAU COMMUNICATIONS SECTION NEW YORK TO DIRECTOR
Att: DID

April 18, 1972
Subject: John Winston Lennon
Security matter: New Left

On April 18, instant, a representative of Immigration and Naturalization Service (INS), 20 West Broadway, NYC, advised that subject and wife Yoko Ono Lennon appeared before Special Inquiry Officer Ira Fieldsteel this date for purpose of deportation hearings. The Lennons were represented by their attorney Leon Wildes of NYC.

Mr Wildes made comments concerning the Lennons' child custody case in Houston, Texas, in which he indicated the child had been abducted by his natural father and that the Lennons were attempting to locate child. The attorney commented that his client felt he was being deported due to his outspoken remarks concerning US policy in south-east Asia. The attorney requested delay so as secure character witnesses to testify on behalf of subject. Wildes read into court record where subject had been appointed on to the President's Council for Drug Abuse and as well on to faculty of NY University in NYC.

Special Inquiry Officer Fieldsteel advised that he would make time available to hear character witnesses and set hearing for May 2 next.

After subject left INS he was met by group of 85 supporters including both radio and television and press representatives. Lennon was observed by a representative of the FBI to make a press release in which he inferred INS was attempting to deport him due to his political ideas and present policy of the US Government as to aliens who speak out against the administration.

ADMINISTRATIVE

ReBuairtel April 10 last. INS representative was Vincent A. Schiano, chief trial attorney. SA who observed subject was SA ***.

For info of Bureau, NYCPD Narcotics Division is aware of subject's recent use of narcotics and is attempting to obtain enough info to arrest both subject and wife Yoko Ono based on PD investigation. NYO following. P.

DIRECTOR FBI TO SACs NEW YORK AND WFO

April 20, 1972

Subject:　　　　John Winston Lennon

Security matter:　New Left

ReNYtel April 18, last. Regarding information furnished by subject's attorney to INS that subject had been appointed to President's Council for Drug Abuse and to faculty of New York University, New York expeditiously conduct discreet inquiries in attempt to corroborate this information. WFO conduct inquiry attempt corroborate subject's alleged appointment President's Council for Drug Abuse, correctly known as National Commission on Marijuana and Drug Abuse. Recipients sutel.

New York advise extent live informant coverage concerning subject and insure any information developed regarding subject's use of narcotics while in US immediately disseminated to pertinent local and Federal narcotics officials.

Note:

Subject, former member of Beatles singing group, allegedly in US to assist organizing disruption of Republican National Convention. He is under deportation proceedings and is attempting to delay deportation mainly due to argument that wife, Yoko Ono, should have custody of child currently in US. At deportation hearing in New York City April 18, 1972, before INS, subject's attorney made statement subject appointed to President's Council for Drug Abuse and to faculty of New York University. Subject illegally in US, and New York and WFO should determine immediately whether statements made by subject's attorney are true.

SAC NEW YORK TO FBI DIRECTOR AND SAC WASHINGTON FIELD

April 21, 1972
Subject: John Winston Lennon
Security matter: New Left

On April 21, instant, a source who is in a position to furnish reliable information advised that subject has been offered a teaching position with New York University (NYU) during the summer. NYU has apparently sent subject a letter requesting his affirmative answer regarding the position, and school officials presume that subject will accept.

ADMINISTRATIVE
Reference Bureau teletype dated April 20, last.
     ***. *** NYO has several sources in a position to furnish information on subject's activities but *** sources do not have personal contact with the subject.
     NYO continuing investigation on subject. LHM follows.

December 1968: With Lennon's son, Julian,
at rehearsals of the 'Rolling Stones Rock 'n' Roll Circus Show'

UNITED STATES (VERNMENT

Memorandum

Felt
Camp~~h~~ll
Ro~~~~
M~~~~n
Bishop
Miller, E.S.
Callahan
Casper
Conrad
Dalbey
Cleveland
Ponder
Bates
Waikart
Walters
Soyars
Tele. Room
Holmes
Gandy

1 – Mr. A. Rosen
1 – Mr. T. E. Bishop

TO : Mr. E. S. Miller   DATE: 4-21-72

1 – Mr. E. S. Miller
1 – Mr. T. J. Smith (Horner)
FROM : R. L. Shackelford
1 – Mr. R. L. Shackelford
1 – Mr. R. L. Pence

SUBJECT: JOHN WINSTON LENNON
SECURITY MATTER – NEW LEFT

CLASSIFIED DECISIONS FINALIZED
BY DEPARTMENT REVIEW COMMITTEE (DRC)   CLASSIFIED DECISIONS FINALIZED
DATE: 2/2/86   BY DEPARTMENT REVIEW COMMITTEE (C
                                               DATE 12/10/9

PURPOSE:

To advise of recent tactics of subject, New Left
sympathizer already in U.S. illegally, to avoid deportation
from the U.S.

BACKGROUND:

Lennon is former member of Beatles singing group in
England who, despite clear ineligibility for U.S. visa due to
conviction in London in 1968 for possession of dangerous drugs
(marijuana), was allowed to re-enter U.S. during 1971 on visitors'
visa due to unexplained intervention by State Department with
Immigration and Naturalization Service (INS). Visas of Lennon
and wife Yoko Ono expired 2-29-72 and since that time INS has
been attempting to deport the Lennons.

(C) He has
come to our attention specifically during 2-72 when information
developed he had donated $75,000 to organization named Election
Year Strategy Information Center, organized to disrupt Republican
National Convention.

On 3-1-72 INS notified Lennons to be out of U.S. by
3-15-72. On 3-16-72 Lennons appeared at INS, New York City, for
deportation proceedings and, through their attorney, won delay
of hearings based on subject's attempt to fight narcotics
conviction in England and wife's attempt to regain custody of
child who is now living in U.S. On 4-18-72 Lennons again
appeared at INS, New York City, during which appearance attorney

100-469910
Enclosures sent 4-25-72
RLP:plm
(7)

REC-70 100-469910-10

☒ MAY 9 1972

CLASSIFIED BY SSA 9803 ADD/JS
REASON:
DECLASSIFY ON

CLASSIFIED BY SSA 5668 SLD
DECLASSIFY ON: 25X

CONTINUED – OVER

R.L. SHACKELFORD TO E.S. MILLER

April 21, 1972
Subject: John Winston Lennon
Security matter: New Left

PURPOSE
To advise of recent tactics of subject, New Left sympathizer already in US illegally, to avoid deportation from the US.

BACKGROUND
Lennon is former member of Beatles singing group in England who, despite clear ineligibility for US visa due to conviction in London in 1968 for possession of dangerous drugs (marijuana), was allowed to re-enter US during 1971 on visitor's visa due to unexplained intervention by State Department with Immigration and Naturalization Service (INS). Visas of Lennon and wife Yoko Ono expired February 29, 1972, and since that time INS has been attempting to deport the Lennons.

***. He has come to our attention specifically during February 1972 when information developed he had donated $75,000 to organization named Election Year Strategy Information Center, organized to disrupt Republican National Convention.

On March 1, 1972, INS notified Lennons to be out of US by March 15, 1972. On March 16, 1972, Lennons appeared at INS, New York City, for deportation proceedings and, through their attorney, won delay of hearings based on subject's attempt to fight narcotics conviction in England and wife's attempt to regain custody of child who is now living in US.

On April 18, 1972, Lennons again appeared at INS, New York City, during which appearance attorney commented that subject felt he was being deported due to his outspoken remarks regarding US policy in south-east Asia. Attorney requested delay so character witnesses could be introduced to testify on behalf of subject. Attorney also read into court record fact subject had been appointed to the President's Council for Drug Abuse, correct name National Commission on Marijuana and Drug Abuse (NCMDA), and to the faculty of New York University, New York City. As a result of these revelations, INS set new hearing date for May 2, 1972, and Lennons left INS to be met by throng of supporters and news media reporters who listened to subject's press release implying he was being deported due to his political ideas and policy of the US Government to deport aliens who speak out against the Administration.

OBSERVATIONS

Irony of subject being appointed to President's Council for Drug Abuse, if true, is overwhelming since subject is currently reported heavy user of narcotics and frequently avoided by even Rennie Davis and Jerry Rubin, convicted Chicago Seven Conspiracy trial defendants, due to his excessive use of narcotics. New York City Police Department currently attempting to develop enough information to arrest both Lennons for narcotics use. WFO has contacted NCMDA under pretext and determined no information available indicating subject has been appointed to NCMDA.

New York Office has confirmed that Lennon has been offered teaching position at New York University for summer of 1972. In view of successful delaying tactics to date, there exists real possibility that subject will not be deported from US in near future and possibly not prior to Republican National Convention. Subject's activities being closely followed and any information developed indicating violation of Federal laws will be immediately furnished to pertinent agencies in effort to neutralize any disruptive activities of subject. Information developed to date has been furnished as received to INS and State Department. Information has also been furnished Internal Security Division of the Department.

ACTION

Attached for approval are letters to Honorable H.R. Haldeman at the White House and acting attorney general with copies to the deputy attorney general and assistant attorney general, Internal Security Division, containing information concerning Lennon.

DIRECTOR FBI TO ACTING ATTORNEY GENERAL

April 25, 1972
Subject: John Winston Lennon
Security matter: New Left

John Winston Lennon is a British citizen and former member of the Beatles singing group. ★★★

Despite his apparent ineligibility for a United States visa due to a conviction in London in 1968 for possession of dangerous drugs, Lennon obtained a visa and entered the United States in 1971. During February 1972 a confidential source, who has furnished reliable information in the past, advised that Lennon had contributed $75,000 to a newly organized New Left group formed to disrupt the Republican National Convention. The visas of Lennon and his wife, Yoko Ono, expired on February 29, 1972, and since that time Immigration and Naturalization Service (INS) has been attempting to deport them.

During the Lennons' most recent deportation hearing at INS, New York, New York, on April 18, 1972, their attorney stated that Lennon felt he was being deported due to his outspoken remarks concerning United States policy in south-east Asia. The attorney requested a delay in order that character witnesses could testify for Lennon, and he then read into the court record that Lennon had been appointed to the President's Council for Drug Abuse (National Commission on Marijuana and Drug Abuse) and to the faculty of New York University, New York, New York.

A second confidential source, who has furnished reliable information in the past, advised that Lennon continues to be a heavy user of narcotics. On April 21, 1972, a third confidential source in a position to furnish reliable information advised that there was no

ASSIFIED BY: ~~XX~~
EASON: 1.5 (b) (d)
ECLASSIFY ON: X 5 X6
CA# CV 83-7720
~~XX~~ 9/25/97
CLASSIFIED BY ~~XXXX~~ JS
DECLASSIFY ON: 25X6
CA#83-1720

CA# 94-1678
MCN/ALT

1 – Mr. A. Rosen
1 – Mr. T. E. Bishop

The Acting Attorney General   April 25, 1972

Director, FBI

1 – Mr. E. S. Miller
1 – Mr. R. L. Shackelford
1 – Mr. T. J. Smith (Horner)
1 – Mr. R. L. Pence

JOHN WINSTON LENNON
SECURITY MATTER – NEW LEFT

9863/RDO/JS
7/2/93
CA#83-1230 Declan on
CLASS. BY 1678 R FD /CAm
4-5-83
1678 RF /K/ 1-16-86

John Winston Lennon is a British citizen and former
member of the Beatles singing group. ~~█████████████~~

b7

~~███████████████████████████~~

(C)

Despite his apparent ineligibility for a United States
visa due to a conviction in London in 1968 for possession of
dangerous drugs, Lennon obtained a visa and entered the United
States in 1971. During February, 1972, a confidential source,
who has furnished reliable information in the past, advised that
Lennon had contributed $75,000 to a newly organized New Left
group formed to disrupt the Republican National Convention. (U)
The visas of Lennon and his wife, Yoko Ono, expired on
February 29, 1972, and since that time Immigration and
Naturalization Service (INS) has been attempting to deport
them. During the Lennons' most recent deportation hearing at
INS, New York, New York, on April 18, 1972, their attorney
stated that Lennon felt he was being deported due to his
outspoken remarks concerning United States policy in Southeast
Asia. The attorney requested a delay in order that character
witnesses could testify for Lennon, and he then read into the
court record that Lennon had been appointed to the President's
Council for Drug Abuse (National Commission on Marijuana and
Drug Abuse) and to the faculty of New York University,
New York, New York. (U)   REC 27 100-469910-6
5 APR 26 1972

A second confidential source, who has furnished
reliable information in the past, advised that Lennon continues
to be a heavy user of narcotics. On April 21, 1972, a third
confidential source in a position to furnish reliable information
advised that there was no information available indicating that (C)

100-469910
RLP:plm
(11)

SEE NOTE PAGE TWO

MAILED 2
APR 26 1972

information available indicating that Lennon has been appointed to the National Commission on Marijuana and Drug Abuse. A fourth confidential source in a position to furnish reliable information advised that Lennon has been offered a teaching position at New York University for the summer of 1972.

This information is also being furnished to the honorable H.R. Haldeman, assistant to the president, at the White House. Pertinent information concerning Lennon is being furnished to the Department of State and INS on a regular basis.

Note:
Classified 'Confidential' since information is contained from ***. First confidential source is ***; second confidential source is ***; third confidential source is pretext inquiry by WFO with ***, National Commission on Marijuana and Drug Abuse, Washington, DC; and fourth confidential source is ***, New York University, New York, New York.

See memorandum R.L. Shackelford to Mr E.S. Miller April 21, 1972, captioned as above, prepared by RPL:plm.

UNITED STATES DEPARTMENT OF JUSTICE – FBI
Milwaukee, Wisconsin

April 26, 1972

Subject: Youth International Party (YIP)
Demonstrations during the Democratic National
Convention, July 1972, Miami, Florida

(Reference is made to Milwaukee memorandum dated April 18, 1972, captioned 'Youth International Party (YIP)' and 'Demonstrations during the Democratic National Convention, July 1972, Miami, Florida').

The Youth International Party, also known as Yippies, is a loosely knit, anti-establishment, revolutionary youth organization formed in New York City in January 1968.

Source, who has furnished reliable information in the past, advised on April 17, 1972, that Shirley Jane Hopper traveled to New York City, from Madison, Wisconsin, on March 2, 1972, until March 6, 1972, to meet with Yippie and Zippie representatives.

The following is an account of that trip furnished by source:

Thursday, March 2, 1972
Jane Hopper took a bus to Chicago and stayed with the *** people. She got up early and went down to Continental Driveaway Company and made arrangements for cars to New York and back. She went to the bus station and picked up John Mattes who came down on the bus that morning.

Friday, March 4, 1972
After picking John up she went and picked up the car which

turned out to be a used squad car that was being sent to Brooklyn for resale.

Saturday, March 4, 1972
They arrived in New York at 3:00 a.m. and went to A.J. Weberman's house at 6 Bleeker Street. After getting some sleep, A.J. went over to Tom Forcade's house to get him up. He came back with Frank Rose, who lives with Tom. They decided to make a Zippie presence at the Stonybrook Conference. Jane drove out there with John, Pat Small and Kathy Morales (who are living with A.J.) and Frank Rose. Pat Small made a plea for the people there to join Zippie and announced that there would be a separate caucus for Zip in another room. The Zips drew off maybe a third of the people there. Most people were stopped by the campus police either coming or going. Hopper was stopped and ID'd while waiting to pick her friends up after the thing broke up.

Sunday, March 5, 1972
Hopper went over to the New York switchboard and made arrangements for Zip announcements to appear in a newsletter they are planning to set up for all the underground switchboards in the next month. She went over to Rex Weiner's house. He is the editor of the *New York Ace*, which is an up-and-coming underground paper. He seems to be an old political hand. He was very glad to see us and proposed a party that night to welcome us to New York, at his newspaper office.

The party started at about 9:00 p.m. so Hopper had time to go eat at Tom Forcade's house. He lives in a real dump at 209 East 5th Street. His office is at 204 West 10th Street (basement). He has no legitimate phone. To call out he taps into a Hungarian person's phone. There is a girl there, name Linda, who acts as a servant for Tom and Frank. Linda's parrot interjects 'Right On' whenever the conversation gets rousing. From there Hopper went to the party. She was introduced to the elite of the radical left. Jerry Rubin rushed up to Jane and begged her to let him be a Zippie. She said we would have to iron out a few differences first and she agreed to meet with him the next day. Jane left with Forcade for a while so John, A.J. and his girl, Ann, mingled for a while. Frank was acting as a chauffeur dressed up in a fancy uniform. Jane got quite drunk and Jerry began to give her trouble about it.

Monday, March 6, 1972

This was Hopper's and John's last day in New York so it was packed with business meetings. Hopper had to take care of delivering the car to Brooklyn. When Hopper got back to A.J.'s Tom was there and they were finalizing plans for the smoke-ins. They are apparently going to take place in 20 states and five foreign countries including England, Netherlands, France, Germany and New Zealand. Debi from the Toronto *Guerrilla* arrived to get a ride back with us as far as Erie, Pennsylvania. They left A.J.'s and went over to Jerry Rubin's house at 156 Prince Street.

Stew Albert was there. Jerry told us that the bad press we were giving him had hurt him badly politically. He said he would be finished in politics unless we patched things up. They replied that they thought he was an asshole. He said that Abbie was coming back next month and that he wouldn't let us kick him around. They told him that they would meet Abbie at the airport and throw him out of the party also. He layed down on the floor close to tears. Stew said they were being too rough on him so they chewed him up in like fashion. Jerry asked us to negotiate with him and we agreed to it. We listed our bitches with him: 1. his superstar ego which enables him to appear to lead us while he does none of the work yet gets the credit; 2. financial deals that have netted him money in the past that he made in the name of Yippie but then used for himself. 3. his bad habits; 4. his feud with Tom and other Zip people. He said that he would do anything and we should just tell him what we wanted. They told him they wanted money and they told him that they wanted him to get signatures for the Armstrong petition. They also told him that we would stop bad-rapping him in accords with how well he performs his assignments. We will make no interferences in his affairs political or otherwise as long as he didn't claim leadership in Zip or Yip. He will have no decision-making powers. If he or Abbie want responsibilities in the new party they will have to earn them like everyone else. The fact that they are superstars and can get coverage of events does not impress us at all. They are a liability within the movement. They have turned too many people off. John and Hopper left for Madison. The only trouble they had on the way home was an incident in Pennsylvania. Their car was identified as having been involved in a burglary. They were stopped for about an hour and then released. They were somewhere around Sharon and Mercer, Pennsylvania.

Jane and John seemed to think that Jerry was losing the friendship of John Lennon. John had thought that he was the center of radical politics and by throwing him out we let the thought enter Lennon's head that perhaps Jerry was washed up. Lennon had a message delivered to us at Stonybrook that he would do an Armstrong benefit if we didn't let it out that he was coming. In other words, it had to be happening on its own steam before he would come. He will also come to the convention if they are peaceful, under the same terms.

FBI – COMMUNICATIONS SECTION
NEW YORK TO DIRECTOR
Att: DID

May 3, 1972

Subject: John Winston Lennon

Security matter: Revolutionary activities

On May 2, last, a representative of Immigration and Naturalization Service (INS), New York City, advised that on previous day,
May 1, last, both Lennon and wife Yoko Ono appeared in New
York City court for purpose of obtaining injunction against INS
deportation proceedings. Scheduled hearing at INS was delayed
until May 9, next. New York court on May 2, last, granted a visa
petition be given to subject and wife.

ADMINISTRATIVE

INS representative is Vincent A. Schiano, chief trial attorney, who
further advised that British authorities have advised that Lennon's
narcotics conviction in England is not likely to be overturned.
Schiano further advised large volume of mail being received by
both supporters and non-supporters of deportation proceedings.
Mayor John Lindsay, New York City, publicly requests INS stop
deportation proceedings as Lennons are 'distinguished artists in
the music field and are asset to US'. Pending.

New York Office following.

John Lennon and Yoko Ono at a news conference at the National Press
Club, Washington, DC, on 28 April 1972 – the day a letter from New
York Mayor John V. Lindsay to the Commissioner of the US Immigration
and Naturalization Service was made public. Lindsay urged that
deportation proceedings against the couple be dropped and that they
be granted resident alien status.

Date received	Received from (name or symbol number)	Received by
5/23/72	████████ (Protect) **b2 b7D**	SA ████████ **b7**

Method of delivery *(check appropriate blocks)*

☐ in person ☐ by telephone ☒ by mail ☐ orally ☐ recording device ☐ written by info

If orally furnished and reduced to writing by Agent:	Date of Report
Date	5/13/72
Dictated _____ to _____	
Transcribed _____ DECLASSIFIED BY **5/2/83** on _____ 1678 RFP/ebm	Date(s) of activity
Authenticated by Informant _____	5/13/72

Brief description of activity or material

Report on Benifit for JOHN LENNON and

structure of NYRU.

b2
b7D

File where original is located if not att ████████

INDIVIDUALS DESIGNATED BY AN ASTERISK (*) ONLY ATTENDED A MEETING AND DID NOT ACTIVELY PARTICIP
VIOLENCE OR REVOLUTIONARY ACTIVITIES WERE NOT DISCUSSED.

☐ Information recorded on a card index by _____ on date _____

Remarks: ▲

All necessary action taken

```
22- New York
    1- ████████              b2,b7D.
    1- 100-          (JOHN LENNON)
    1- 100-174832 (ATTICA DEFENSE COMMITTEE)
    1- 100-156088 (ASIAN INFO OFFICE)
    1- ████████
    1- ████████                          CLASS. BY 1678 RFP/ebm
    1- ████████                                          5.2.83
    1- ████████                          declas DADR
    1- ████████
b7c 1- ████████                          ALL INFORMATION CONTAINED
    1- ████████                          HEREIN IS UNCLASSIFIED EXCEPT
    1- ████████                          WHERE SHOWN OTHERWISE.
    1- ████████
    1- ████████
    1- 100-174986 (NYRC)
```

Copies Continued.

b7c ████████

(22)   CLASS. & EXT. BY ████████
       REASON FCIM II, 1-2.4.?
       DATE OF REVIEW 6/6/97

6/22/82

Block Stamp

100 - 175319

SEARCHED _____ FILED _____
SERIALIZED _____ FILED _____
42
████████ NEW YORK

CONFIDENTIAL

INFORMANT REPORT OF MAY 13, 1972

Received May 23, 1972
Prepared June 6, 1972
Subject: Report on benefit for John Lennon and structure of
  NYRU

After John Lennon plugged it on the Dick Cavett Show, the benefit concert for the Attica Defense Committee turned a larger crowd than expected. Among the people who came were Otto Preminger and a party of 5 people. Security was tight. The AIO core group included Ronald Rosen, Josephine Pizzino (both new members of AIO), James Duffy, Maurice Wade, and was led by Walter Teague. Also on security were Walter Aponti (recently purged from AIO) Lawrence Remer, Diane Danham and Stephen Pomepante. The benefit was held at the Washington Square Methodist Church (WSMC), began at about 20:00, was ended about 1:30 Sunday morning by a bomb threat, and netted $2,000 for the Defense Committee and $200 for the WSMC.

At 15:00 the NYRC had a meeting on re-organization at its HQ (98B Third Ave.). The meeting was fruitless. The two factions are basically these: Lawrence Levy and Henry Platsky want to form a more intellectually oriented group which functions as a study group, at least at the outset. Robert Henes, Eugenie S. Joseph, Susan Lnu, William Smith, Lester Baum and some unidentified members of the Prison Collective (an arm of NYRC concerned with prisoner liaison) wish the group to become more action oriented, feeling that any form of movement toward the study group idea is a cowardly retreat.

Other facts:
★★★ . ★★★

May 16, 1972

Subject: John Winston Lennon

Security matter: Revolutionary activities

ReNYtel May 3, last.

On May 16, instant, Vincent Schiano, chief trial attorney, INS, NYC, advised subject and wife, Yoko Ono, are scheduled for hearing on deportation proceedings May 17, next.

Schiano advised INS using three key points for hearing next:

One, concerning child custody case of Kyoko Cox, son of Anthony David Cox and Yoko Ono by previous marriage. Lennons claim natural father abducted son shortly after court in Houston, Texas, awarded Lennons custody with requirements child be raised in US. INS believes Lennons and Cox may be party to keeping child hidden as tool of delaying deportation hearings. If fact established, INS will go on perjury charges against Lennons.

★★★. ★★★

Three, INS will request mental examination of Lennons at later date.

PAGE TWO

PARTY TO KEEPING CHILD HIDDEN AS TOOL OF DELAYING DEPORTATION

HEARINGS.   IF FACT ESTABLISHED, INS WILL GO ON PERJURY

CHARGES AGAINST LENNONS.
                    Immigration and Naturalization Service

b3

        THREE, INS WILL REQUEST MENTAL EXAMINATION OF LENNONS

AT LATER DATE.

END

PLS ACK FOR THREE
ACK FOR THREE TELS   T's to Rosen
                                         Miller
MRF FBI WA DC   Wannall
                                         Shackelford
                                         Recer

DOMESTIC INTELLIGENCE DIVISION
Informative Note

May 17, 1972

You were previously advised that both John Lennon and his wife, Yoko Ono, are in the US and that Lennon is the major financial contributor to the Election Year Strategy Information Center (EYSIC) which was organized to conduct disruptive demonstrations during the Republican National Convention. EYSIC has been 'dying on the vine' due to Lennon's possible deportation which he is fighting in court.

Lennon and his wife have been fighting deportation proceedings in New York City. Attached states that Lennon and his wife are scheduled for deportation proceedings on May 17, 1972, in New York City. INS planning to utilize two key points during the hearing as follows: (1) establish claims by the Lennons that child was abducted by natural father are false; (2) establish that Lennon's claim he earned no income while in US involves fraud. INS plans to request mental examination of both Lennons.

For information.

Yoko Ono, John Lennon and Yoko's daughter, Kyoko Cox, May 1969

JOHN AND YOKO JOINING VIGIL HERE
New York Post, May 19, 1972

A weekend of massive demonstrations has been scheduled to take place here and across the country by several peace groups demanding complete withdrawal of US forces from Indochina.

A candlelight vigil and 'procession for peace' tomorrow night in Duffy Square, at Broadway between 46th and 47th Streets, from 8 to 11 p.m., will highlight local activities.

Sponsored by the National Peace Action Coalition the vigil is expected to attract a number of prominent members of the city's art community, and rally support for massive demonstration scheduled for Washington on Sunday.

The two demonstrations were announced by NPAC National Coordinator Katherine Sojourner yesterday.

Supporters of the Sunday march in Washington include about 25 members of Congress, a number of local politicians, and trade union leaders from across the country.

JOHN AND YOKO

Members of the art community endorsing the Washington march and expected to attend tomorrow's vigil include John Lennon and Yoko Ono; satirist Jules Feiffer; producer Joseph Papp; writers Arthur Miller and William Styron and others.

'This Sunday in Washington, thousands of Americans will express their opposition to Nixon's latest and most dangerous escalations', said novelist Kurt Vonnegut, Jr, reading a statement signed by about 50 prominent artists.

'At this critical time, we believe it important to share some time and feeling for peace', the statement said.

On Monday, Washington demonstrators plan what they call a

'blockade' of the Pentagon by blocking entrances to the building.

Plans were also announced today by the US Servicemen's Fund, for a series of anti-war demonstrations at Fort Dix and more than 30 other military bases and installations across the country tomorrow. Similar Armed Forces Day demonstrations organized by active-duty military personnel last year have forced the Pentagon to cancel official parades and ceremonies at these bases.

Such fears by officials of the Military Order of the World Wars resulted in the cancellation of New York's 23rd annual Armed Forces Day parade this week.

MILTON ADAMS

FBI COMMUNICATIONS SECTION
NEW YORK TO ACTING DIRECTOR
Att: DID Houston

May 23, 1972
Subject: John Winston Lennon
Security matter: Revolutionary activities (origin: New York)

Re New York tel to Bureau May 18, last. Houston not in receipt of referenced tel.

For information of Houston, subject and wife Yoko Ono involved in anti-war activities and plan to travel to Republican and Democratic Convention this year. INS attempting to deport both Lennons on grounds of subject's 1968 narcotic conviction in England.

Lennons using delay tactics in deportation of attempting to locate Yoko Ono's child Kyoko Cox, who was reported abducted by natural father Anthony David Cox. Houston court has awarded custody of child to Lennons. No process out on Cox.

NYO in receipt of information this date that Lennons have hidden child at residence of *** in attempts to delay deportation.

INS has advised they will file perjury charges against Lennons if established Lennon furnished false information during INS hearing.

LEAD
Houston: At *** conduct appropriate investigation to determine if Kyoko Cox is at above address, and attempt to establish if *** in contact with Lennons in NYC. Sutel.

May 1971: Vietnam veterans participating in the 'May Day' demonstration – conceived to be a total disruption of Washington, DC, as a protest against continued US involvement in Vietnam

2/13/96

CLASSIFIED BY: SSA 9803RDD/JS
REASON: 1.5 (b)
DECLASSIFY ON: X 5

TELETYPE

CODE

CA# CV83-1720   CA# 83-1720

CLASSIFIED DECISIONS FINALIZED
BY DEPARTMENT REVIEW COMMITTEE (DRC)
DATE: 12/16/97 SSA SLD/JS 12/16/97

IMMEDIATE

5/24/72

TO   SACS NEW YORK (100-175319)
      HOUSTON

FROM ACTING DIRECTOR FBI (100-469910) - 14

1 - Mr. C.W. Bates
      (C.A. Nuzum)
1 - Mr. R.L. Shackelford
1 - Mr. R.L. Pence

JOHN WINSTON LENNON, SM - REVOLUTIONARY ACTIVITIES.

RENYTEL MAY TWENTY-THREE LAST.

CLASSIFIED DECISIONS FINALIZED
BY DEPARTMENT REVIEW COMMITTEE (DRC)
DATE: 2/2/96   1678 LFP   3/8/96

HOUSTON DISREGARD LEAD SET BY NEW YORK IN REFERENCED TELETYPE

EXCEPT FOR CONTACT WITH ESTABLISHED SOURCES ONLY.

BUREAU FULLY AWARE PROGRESS OF NEW YORK OFFICE IN DEVELOPING

EXCELLENT COVERAGE SUBJECT'S ACTIVITIES, HOWEVER, ASPECTS INVESTI-

GATION RELATING TO SUBJECT'S APPEARANCE AT INS HEARINGS AND POSSIBLE

PERJURY INVOLVED IN FALSE STATEMENTS MADE BY SUBJECT STRICTLY

RESPONSIBILITY OF INS. INFORMATION DEVELOPED BY NEW YORK SHOULD BE

IMMEDIATELY, IF NOT ALREADY, FURNISHED TO INS. ALL SUBSEQUENT

INFORMATION DEVELOPED REGARDING SUBJECT'S VIOLATIONS OF FEDERAL AND

LOCAL LAWS INCLUDING NARCOTICS OR PERJURY, SHOULD LIKEWISE BE

DISSEMINATED WITHOUT DELAY TO PERTINENT AGENCIES.

JTR RLP:mcm   (CLASS. BY 1678 RFP/EBm   CLASS. & EXT. BY
9803RDD   NOTE: Declass on   REASON: FIM II, 1-2, 4.2
7/2/72   05   1678 RFP/JS 1-16-86   DATE OF REVIEW 5/9/
CA# 83-1720

Lennon is former member of Beatles singing group in
England who, despite clear ineligibility for U.S. visa due to
narcotics conviction in England in 1968 was allowed to reenter
U.S. during 1971 on visitors visa. Visas of Lennon and wife, Yoko
Ono, expired 2/72 and since that time Immigration and Naturalization
Service (INS) has been attempting to deport Lennons. New York
Office following activities of Lennon closely ████████████████ b1

████████████████████████████████ Information developed by our

Tolson
Felt
Campbell
Rosen
Mohr
Bishop
Miller, E.S.
Callahan
Casper
Conrad
Dalbey
Cleveland
Ponder
Bates
Walkart
Walters
Soyars
Tele. Room
Holmes
Gandy

COMMUNICATIONS SECTION
MAY 24 1972

70 JUN 6 1972

MAIL ROOM   TELETYPE UNIT

NOTE CONTINUED - OVER

ALL INFORMATION CONTAINED
HEREIN IS UNCLASSIFIED EXCEPT
WHERE SHOWN OTHERWISE

ACTING DIRECTOR FBI TO SACs
NEW YORK AND HOUSTON

May 24, 1972
Subject: John Winston Lennon
Security matter: Revolutionary activities

ReNYtel May 23, last.

Houston disregard lead set by New York in referenced teletype except for contact with established sources only.

Bureau fully aware progress of New York Office in developing excellent coverage subject's activities. However, aspects investigation relating to subject's appearance at INS hearing and possible perjury involved in false statements made by subject strictly responsibility of INS. Information developed by New York should be immediately, if not already, furnished to INS. All subsequent information developed regarding subject's violations of Federal and local laws, including narcotics or perjury, should likewise be disseminated without delay to pertinent agencies.

Note:

Lennon is former member of Beatles singing group in England who, despite clear ineligibility for US visa due to narcotics conviction in England in 1968, was allowed to re-enter US during 1971 on visitor's visa. Visas of Lennon and wife, Yoko Ono, expired February 1972 and since that time Immigration and Naturalization Service (INS) has been attempting to deport Lennons. New York Office following activities of Lennon closely ***. Information developed by our sources that Lennon donated $75,000 to organization formed to disrupt Republican National Convention. Lennons using delaying tactics to avoid deportation,

claiming that they must locate Ono's child by former marriage who was reported abducted by natural father Anthony Cox. New York developed information that Lennons actually have child hidden at certain residence in Houston division for purpose of delaying deportation. INS considering filing perjury charges against Lennons if information can be established they furnished false information during hearing. New York has set urgent lead for Houston division to attempt to locate Ono's child and attempt to establish if person keeping child is in contact with Lennons. Actual location of Ono's child and subsequent prosecution for perjury in this instance is responsibility of INS and Houston being instructed to disregard lead except for contact with established sources only. In view of possible court proceedings, active investigation by FBI in this area could result in FBI agents testifying, which would not be in Bureau's best interest and could result in considerable adverse publicity.

A Vietnam veteran attending an anti-Vietnam War rally at Valley Forge, Pennsylvania (1970)

SAC NEW YORK TO ACTING DIRECTOR FBI

May 25, 1972
Subject: John Winston Lennon
Security matter: Revolutionary activities

ReButel and Houston teletype, both dated May 24, 1972.

On May 25, 1972, Mr Vincent Schiano, chief trial attorney, INS, NYC, advised that his agency is in receipt of a letter from *** dated May 19, 1972, which states the following:

> I can no longer remain silent, I know the whereabouts of Kyoko Cox, and I wish to be of assistance. I am willing to help. ...

The letter was signed ***.

Schiano advised that he will contact his headquarters in Washington this date and advise the appropriate official, Mr Carl Burrows, who is in charge of INS investigation of the above information. He will request INS officials in Texas to contact *** concerning her letter.

Schiano also advised that he has considered requesting INS to place the subject and Yoko Ono on bond pending the outcome of their deportation proceedings and to restrict their travel. He has received information that the Lennons are planning a large rock concert in Miami during the conventions and that the rock concert was to be held in front of the Convention Hall.

The above information is being furnished in view of possibility *** may contact the Houston office. *** name should be appropriately indexed.

Transmit the following in _____

(Type in plaintext or code)

Via _____ AIRTEL

(Priority)

TO: ACTING DIRECTOR, FBI (100-469910)

FROM: SAC, NEW YORK (100-175319) (P)

SUBJECT: JOHN WINSTON LENNON
          SM-REVOLUTIONARY ACTIVITIES
          (OO:NY)

        ReButel and Houston teletype both dated 5/24/72.

        On 5/25/72, Mr. VINCENT SCHIANO, Chief Trial
Attorney, INS, NYC, advised that his agency is in receipt
of a letter from █████████████████████████████ dated
5/19/72, which states the following: **b7c**

        "I can no longer remain silent, I know the where-
abouts of KYOKO COX, and I wish to be of assistance. I am
willing to help..."

        The letter was signed ███████████ **b7c**

        SCHIANO advised that he will contact his headquarter
in Washington this date and advise the appropriate official,
Mr. CARL BURROWS, who is in charge of INS Investigation of
the above information. He will request INS officials in
Texas to contact ████████ concerning her letter.

b7c

2 - Bureau (RM)
1 - Houston (INFO) (RM)
3 - Miami (RM)
   (1 - MIDEM)
   (1 - MIREP)
1 - New York
CJL:slb
(8)

REC-170

100-469910- 15

ALL INFORMATION CONTAINED
HEREIN IS UNCLASSIFIED
DATE 2/12/81 BY SP4/SRm/mc

■ MAY 27 1972

51 JUN 1 1972

Approved: _____   Sent _____ M Per _____
    Special Agent in Charge

CANDLELIGHT VIGIL AND PROCESSION FOR PEACE

STOP THE BLOCKADE NOW!
STOP THE BOMBING NOW!
US OUT OF SE ASIA NOW!

This Sunday in Washington thousands of Americans of all ages will express their opposition – legally and peacefully – to Nixon's latest and most dangerous escalation. At this critical time we members of New York's community of the arts believe it important to share with you some time and feeling for peace.

Join us Saturday night, May 20, 1972 – 8 to 11 p.m. in Duffy Square. And, remember, you … we … are not alone!

Rae Allen	Lee Grant	John Lennon and Yoko Ono	Muriel Rukeyser
David Amram	Tammy Grimes	Viveca Lindfore	Janice Rule
Peter Boyle	John Hammond	Paul Lipson	Robert Ryan
Joseph Chaikin	Barbara Harris	Helen Lynd	Isiah Sheffer
Gavin Cort	Jon Hendricks	Monica McCall	William Styron
Ossie Davis	Jules Irving	Charles Maryan	Barbara Tarbuck
Ruby Dee	Anne Jackson	Arthur Miller	Harold Taylor
Jules Feiffer	Jill Krementz	Anais Nin	Jean-Claude Van Italie
Gene Frankel	John Lahr	Jerry & Marta Orbach	Kurt Vonnegut Jr
Ben Gazzara	Lynn and Burton Lane	Joseph Papp	Gerald and Greta Walker
Bernard Gersten	Madeline Lee	Estelle Parsons	Eli Wallach
Jack Gilford			

MARCH ON WASHINGTON INFORMATION

TRANSPORTATION

Bus tickets: $10 round trip. Train tickets: $15 round trip. Buses leave Manhattan, Queens, Brooklyn, Bronx at 6:00 a.m. Buses leave DC at 6:00 p.m. Train leaves Penn Station at 7:00 a.m., and leaves DC at 6:00 p.m. Make checks payable to 'NPAC TRANSPORTATION FUND'.

DEMONSTRATION DETAILS

Assemble:10:00 a.m. at the Ellipse.

March: Noon on Pennsylvania Avenue.

Rally: 1:00 p.m. on the Capitol Steps, west side.

For more information, to volunteer, or to purchase tickets, contact: NATIONAL PEACE ACTION COALITION, 150 Fifth Avenue, New York, NY 10011. (212) 741-2018. Urgent – we need money now to help pay for Ma---.

UNITED STATES GOVERNMENT

Memorandum

TO : SAC, New York (100-170471)　████ SECRET 6/2/72

FROM : SA ████████████████████　b7c

SUBJECT: NATIONAL PEACE ACTION COALITION
(NPAC)
IS-C (TROTSKYIST)
OO: NY.

The attached flyer was obtained from unidentified individual by SA ████████████████ at an anti-war Demonstration on 5/20/72 at Duffy Sq, NYC, NY.

CLASS. & EXT. BY ████ 4/19/82

REASON-FCIM II 1-2.4.2 (2) (3)

DATE OF REVIEW ████

DO NOT DESTROY — PENDING LITIGATION

100-170471-1360

DECLASSIFIED ON 5-3-83

BY 1678 RFP/SBm

SECRET

SEARCHED
SERIALIZED
b7c

AIRTEL
SAC MIAMI TO ACTING DIRECTOR FBI

June 5, 1972

Subject: John Winston Lennon

Security matter: Revolutionary activities

Office of origin: New York

MIDEM

Re New York airtel to the Bureau dated May 25, 1972, under first caption above.

New York airtel indicated information was received from Vincent Schiano, chief trial attorney, INS, New York City, on May 25, 1972, to the effect that he had received information that subject Lennon and his wife, Yoko Ono, are planning a large rock concert in Miami during the conventions and that the rock concert was to be held in front of the Convention Hall.

LEAD

At New York, New York: Will re-contact Attorney Schiano for source and accuracy of above information. New York thereafter requested to place this information in LHM form under caption Demonstration at Democratic and Republican National Convention.

John Lennon and Yoko Ono outside the Dakota apartments, Manhattan, New York – the photo that appeared on his last record album, *Double Fantasy*

JOHN & YOKO WAIT & WAIT
Daily News, July 14, 1972

A decision in the deportation proceedings against former Beatle John Lennon and his Japanese-born wife, Yoko Ono, may not be reached until September, the US Immigration and Naturalization Service said yesterday.

The Government and Defense were to have submitted briefs by July 1, but they are still waiting for a transcript of the May 17 hearing.

Special Inquiry Officer Ira Fieldsteel, who is hearing the case, will be away in August, and so a decision is not expected until September.

The Government wants to deny Lennon permanent residence here because of a 1968 marijuana conviction in England.

August 1980: John Lennon and Yoko Ono entering The Hit Factory, Manhattan, New York, to begin closed recording sessions on their first album in seven years

Transmit the following in _____

(Type in plaintext or code)

Via ____ AIRTEL _____

DECLASSIFIED ON 4-27-84
BY 1678 RFP/EBm

TO: ACTING DIRECTOR, FBI)(100-469910)

FROM: SAC, NEW YORK (100-175319) (P)

SUBJECT: JOHN WINSTON LENNON
SM - REVACT
(OO: NY)

CLASS. BY 1678 RFP/EBm
4.5.83
Declass on [ ]

MIREP

ReNYairtel, dated 5/25/72, and Miami airtel, dated 6/5/72,

Attached are 5 copies for the Bureau, and seven copies for Miami, of an LHM dated and captioned as above.

Miami should note that LENNON is reportedly a "heavy user of narcotics" known as "downers". This information should be emphasized to local Law Enforcement Agencies covering MIREP, with regards to subject being arrested if at all possible on possession of narcotics charge.

Local INS has very loose case in NY for deporting subject on narcotics charge involving 1968 arrest in England.

INS has stressed to Bureau that if LENNON were to be arrested in US for possession of narcotics he would become more likely to be immediately deportable.

ST-111
REC-5   100-469910-18

2 - Bureau (Encls. 5) (RM)
2 - Miami (Encls. 7) (RM)
1 - New York

25 JUL 29 1972

CJL:lbr
(6)

ENCLOSURE

REO REC.D

Approved: _____ Sent _____ M Per _____
Special Agent in Charge

61 AUG 2 1972

XEROX

SAC NEW YORK TO ACTING DIRECTOR FBI

July 27, 1972
Subject: John Winston Lennon
Security matter: Revact

ReNYairtel, dated May 25, 1972, and Miami airtel, dated June 5, 1972.

Attached are five copies for the Bureau, and seven copies for Miami, of an LHM dated and captioned as above.

Miami should note that Lennon is reportedly a 'heavy user of narcotics' known as 'downers'. This information should be emphasized to local Law Enforcement Agencies covering MIREP, with regards to subject being arrested if at all possible on possession of narcotics charge.

Local INS has very loose case in NY for deporting subject on narcotics charge involving 1968 arrest in England.

INS has stressed to Bureau that if Lennon were to be arrested in US for possession of narcotics he would become more likely to be immediately deportable.

Captioned LHM is classified 'Confidential' because it contains information furnished by confidential sources *** through *** who are of continuing value; the unauthorized disclosure of which information would lend to identify them and thus be prejudicial to the national defense interest of the US.

LHM is so classified by SA ***.

SAC SAN FRANCISCO TO ACTING DIRECTOR FBI

August 1, 1972

Subject:	Rainbow People's Party (formerly the White Panther Party)
Security matter:	IS – WPP
Office of Origin:	Detroit

Enclosed for Detroit is a xeroxed copy of the May 19, 1972, issue of *Grass Roots*, self-described as the National Publication of the People's Party, which has its national office at 140 M Street NW, Washington, DC 20005. Enclosed item was xeroxed from a copy made available by *** on *** as having been received by ***. Xeroxed copy of this and other items made available by *** were furnished to the Bureau, WFO and St Louis by SF letter to Bureau dated July 31, 1972, captioned 'People's Party, IS – New Left'.

Although enclosed item undoubtedly received wide distribution and needs no classification, any mention that it was received by *** must be classified to protect the sensitive relations between *** and such mention should be avoided since ***.

Enclosed item sets forth an article by Lowell Young, captioned 'A time of trial for the People's Party', in which he deplores the fact that some potential and actual supporters of the People's Party have decided to support McGovern's candidacy. Lowell spends some time discussing the captioned organization and its having united with the Youth International Party and deplores the fact that 'Abbie Hoffman, Jerry Rubin, John Sinclair, Genie Plamondon and the entire Rainbow People's Party of Michigan have come out in support of George McGovern's candidacy'.

Memorandum

TO : ACTING DIRECTOR, FBI (62-112678)   DATE: 8/1/72

FROM : SAC, SAN FRANCISCO (100-61875) CONFIDENTIAL

CLASS. & EXT. BY
REASON-FCIM II, 1-2.4.2
DATE OF REVIEW 8/1/92

Classified by
Declassify on: OADR

SUBJECT: RAINBOW PEOPLE'S PARTY
(formerly the White Panther Party)
IS - WPP

OO: DETROIT

Enclosed for Detroit is a xeroxed copy of the May 19, 1972 issue of "GRASS ROOTS", self described as the National Publication of the People's Party, which has its National Office at 140½ M Street NW, Washington, D.C. 20005. Enclosed item was xeroxed from a copy made available by [redacted] on [redacted] as having been Received by [redacted] Xeroxed copy of this and other items made available by [redacted] were furnished to the Bureau, WFO and St. Louis by SF Letter to Bureau dated 7/31/72, captioned: PEOPLE'S PARTY, IS - NEW LEFT. (b2) (b7D)

Although enclosed item undoubtedly received wide distribution and needs no classification, any mention that it was received by [redacted] must be classified to protect the sensitive relationship between [redacted] and such mention should be avoided, since [redacted]

NO LOCALITY (b2) (b7D)

Enclosed item, on pages 10 through 13 sets forth an article by LOWELL YOUNG, captioned:"A TIME OF TRIAL FOR THE PEOPLE'S PARTY", in which he deplores the fact that some potential and actual supporters of the People's Party have decided to support McGovern's candidacy. LOWELL spends some time discussing the captioned organization and its having united with the Youth International Party and deplores the fact that"ABBIE HOFFMAN, JERRY RUBIN, JOHN SINCLAIR, GENIE PLAMONDON"and the entire Rainbow People's Party of Michigan have come out in support of George McGovern's candidacy". YOUNG's article appears to be of interest and is set out in xeroxed form as the following four pages of instant letter.

6 - Bureau (RM)
(2 - 62-112678)
(2 - 100-448910; Y.I.P.)
(1 - 105-184368; RU)
(1 - [redacted]
3 - Detroit (100-36217) (RM)
3 - New York (RM)
(1 - 100-162260; Y.I.P.)
4 - San Francisco (1 - 100-61875)
(1 - 100-61692; Y.I.P.) (1 - 100-61281; RU)
(1 - [redacted]
JES/jes
(16)

(b2) (b7D)

EX 101

DECLASSIFIED ON 4-27-94

REC-59

62-112678-359

CONFIDENTIAL

4 AUG 9 1972

105-118969

A TIME OF TRIAL FOR THE PEOPLE'S PARTY
Grass Roots, May 19, 1972

> My candidacy is the only way to avoid a fourth party on the left in 1972. (George McGovern)

The George McGovern candidacy for the Democratic nomination for president has been transformed from an invisible campaign supported by only a faithful few into a lavishly financed campaign of a front-runner. From the beginning, McGovern's campaign has been an attempt to co-opt a fourth party on the left by adopting the left's issues and rhetoric as his own. His initial strong stands in opposition to the war and in favor of amnesty for all draft evaders and exiles, legalization of marijuana, abortion on demand, and the shifting of the burden of taxation from the poor and the working class on to the shoulders of the super-rich and the corporations were all designed to rally all possible fourth party constituents to his cause. And, for the moment, he has partially succeeded.

Recently, Abbie Hoffman, Jerry Rubin, John Sinclair, Genie Plamondon and the entire Rainbow People's Party of Michigan have come out in support of George McGovern's candidacy. Abbie Hoffman and Jerry Rubin founded the Youth International Party (YIP) in early 1967. Their perfection of the use of guerrilla theater was designed to gain media attention in order to try to educate the American people about the hypocrisy of the present system.

To strengthen their organization and broaden their base of support, they united YIP with the Michigan-based White Panther Party. The White Panther Party was founded by John Sinclair and Plamondon with the aim of it becoming the white counterpart of the Black Panther Party. But that never came to be due to the different forms of oppression the different constituencies of the

Above December 1980, Central Park, New York:
At a memorial service for John Lennon
Below 12 December 1980, Washington, DC: A group of protesters
in a demonstration sponsored by Citizens Against Violence
outside the National Rifle Association

Black and White Panther Parties are subjected to. Black people are oppressed racially and materially; so the 10-point program of the Black Panther Party related to those forms of political oppression by making political demands for 'land, bread, housing, clothing, education, justice, and peace'. The white people Sinclair and Plamondon were attempting to organize were primarily culture-oriented; so the 10-point program of the White Panther Party related primarily to their cultural oppression by demanding an open society where free dope, free sex and free rock music abounded. (They did make political references as well, the principal ones being the right of armed self-defense and complete support for the 10-point program of the Black Panther Party.)

While their followers were primarily culturally oriented, Sinclair and Plamondon were themselves very political. They were thought to believe that the perverted system of values in this country was a direct outgrowth of the undemocratic political system and the competitive economic system. By primarily relating to their followers' cultural oppression now, they supposedly hoped to educate them to the system's role in that oppression later. They were therefore viewed as very dangerous by the power structure and were moved against. Plamondon was framed on a charge of attempting to blow up a Federal building in Ann Arbor and is still in jail today. Sinclair was given a 10-year jail sentence for possessing two joints and wasn't released until early this spring.

The Rainbow People's Party was founded by Sinclair as the successor to the White Panther Party. It concentrated its efforts on local community organizing in the Ann Arbor area and linked up with the state-wide Human Rights Party. Five Rainbow candidates, including 'Pun' Plamondon's wife Genie, ran for Ann Arbor city council seats in April under the Human Rights Party banner. Part of the agreement between the two parties was that neither would support any Democratic candidates. But, two weeks after two of their candidates got elected, Sinclair, Genie Plamondon and the rest of the Rainbow Party broke the agreement and announced their support for George McGovern.

But they are not alone. Such 'radical' entertainers as Joan Baez and John Lennon have also come out in support of McGovern. Also, Gore Vidal, secretary of state in the People's Party shadow cabinet, and an individual with the means to provide the party with much-needed economic assistance, never came across with a cent, and at the May 4 moratorium rally in New York City announced his support for George McGovern.

The defections by potential members and, worse yet, by people within the party itself, make this a period of extreme darkness for the People's Party. But, that proverbial light at the end of the tunnel is coming into view; and the reason is George McGovern himself.

As his chances of getting the nomination have become better, McGovern has found it necessary to broaden his base of support by moving to the right. He is making an attempt to win over the reactionary labor leaders currently in the Humphrey camp. He is talking more about the economic issues relevant to George Wallace's alienated constituency than about the political or cultural issues relevant to his own alienated constituency.

George McGovern has a history of backing off on strong stands he might initially take. He initially agreed to introduce a bill on the floor of the Senate calling for statehood for the colony of Columbia, but at the last moment changed his mind, much to the embarrassment and anger of Julius Hobson and the DC Statehood Party. He initially agreed to run a slate of delegates in Chicago as a challenge to Mayor Daley in the Illinois Primary, but, after a 20-minute talk in the mayor's office, agreed not to challenge Daley, much to the chagrin of his Chicago supporters. During the recent Nebraska primary, McGovern was accused of harboring 'radical' views regarding the issues of marijuana, amnesty and abortion. He immediately changed his previously stated positions. Now, he is opposed to the legalization of marijuana, says that abortion is a matter for the states to deal with, and that all draft evading cases should be dealt with on an individual basis.

'Radicals' who support George McGovern do not have a clear understanding of the true nature of this society and the ruling system responsible for the current oppressive conditions. We in the People's Party have a general understanding of the problem, but by no means do we possess a specific or a clearly thought out understanding to the point that we can serve as that force which will educate and awaken the unconscious and mislead (by McGovern on down) masses of the American people.

In order to develop that specific and clearly thought out understanding, we must turn our energies inward, i.e., concentrate on educating those of us already committed to building the People's Party so that we can begin to make crystal clear the differences between what we must advocate and the 'New Populism' of George McGovern and the left wing of the Democratic Party. They advocate reforming the present capitalist system; we must advocate replacing the present capitalist system with socialism. But, in order to talk about socialism to others, we must first have a complete understanding of socialism ourselves.

Our attempts at recruitment should center upon those groups and individuals politically educated enough to contribute to this period of internal development. This doesn't mean that we should be closed to those who through their own bitter experience decide that they should join the party. In the immediate future, as McGovern's move to the right – and thus his duplicity – becomes more blatant, the People's Party can expect an influx of McGovern's more radical supporters, including, hopefully, all those mentioned above. The doors should and will be open to them.

John Lennon, c.1967

The further one looks into the future the brighter that light at the end of the darkness becomes. If McGovern gets the nomination, wins the election and then proceeds to carry on Johnson's and Nixon's policies (since he can't do any different because of the nature of the system), then for many millions of the American people that will be it. They will be through with the Democratic Party and the capitalist system, and they will turn to the only mass-based, independent political party calling for socialism: the People's Party!

LOWELL YOUNG

TO : ACTING DIRECTOR, FBI (100-469910) DATE: 8/30/72

FROM : SAC, NEW YORK (100-175319) (P*)

SUBJECT: JOHN WINSTON LENNON
SM-REVACT
(OO: NY)

DECLASSIFIED ON 4-27-34
BY 1678 RFp/Eom

Re NY airtel and LHM, 7/27/72.

Referenced communications set forth background information as requested by Miami in view of MIREP activities in that city, August 21-24, 1972.

Case Agent traveled to Miami as a member of the Weatherman Task Group (WTG). The subject was not observed by the case agent and based on informant coverage it is believed that the subject did not travel to Miami for the Republican National Convention as he had previously planned.

On August 28, 1972, Mr. VINCENT SCHIANO, Chief Trial Attorney, INS, NYC, advised that no information has come to his attention to indicate the subject traveled to Miami.

For the past several months there has been no information received to indicate that the subject is active in the New Left.

Sources; ██████████████████████████████ all advised during the month of July, 1972, that the subject has fallen out of the favor of activist JERRY RUBIN, STEWART ALBERT, and RENNIE DAVIS, due to subject's lack of interest in committing himself to involvement in anti-war and New Left activities.

In view of this information the New York Division is placing this case in a pending inactive status. When information concerning subject's tentative deportation is received such information will be sent to the Bureau.

2-Bureau (RM)
1-New York

REC-24   100-469910-20

CJL:jas
(3)

EX-104

21 SEP 1 1972

54 SEP 19 1972

CLASS. & EXT. BY Sp █/5 █████
REASON-FCIM II, 1-2.4.2 █
DATE OF REVIEW 5/30/83

SAC NEW YORK TO ACTING DIRECTOR FBI

August 30, 1972

Subject: John Winston Lennon

Security matter: Revact

Re NY airtel and LHM, July 27, 1972.

Referenced communications set forth background information as requested by Miami in view of MIREP activities in that city, August 21–24, 1972.

Case Agent traveled to Miami as a member of the Weatherman Task Group (WTG). The subject was not observed by the case agent and based on informant coverage it is believed that the subject did not travel to Miami for the Republican National Convention as he had previously planned.

On August 28, 1972, Mr Vincent Schiano, chief trial attorney, INS, NYC, advised that no information has come to his attention to indicate the subject traveled to Miami.

For the past several months there has been no information received to indicate that the subject is active in the New Left.

Sources *** *** all advised during the month of July 1972 that the subject has fallen out of the favor of activist Jerry Rubin, Stewart Albert and Rennie Davis, due to subject's lack of interest in committing himself to involvement in anti-war and New Left activities.

In view of this information the New York Division is placing this case in a pending inactive status. When information concerning subject's tentative deportation is received such information will be sent to the Bureau.

Memorandum

TO : Acting Director, FBI

DATE: 9/12/72

FROM : Legat, London (105-5492) (P)

SUBJECT: JOHN WINSTON LENNON
SM-NEW LEFT

OO - NYC

~~SECRET~~

9/25/97
CLASSIFIED BY SSA 5668 SLD/JS
DECLASSIFY ON: 25X 6
CA # 83-1720

CLASSIFIED DECISIONS FINALIZED
BY DEPARTMENT REVIEW COMMITTEE (DRC)
DATE: 2/2/86   1678 [P] --- 3/8/86

CLASSIFIED DECISIONS FINALIZED
BY DEPARTMENT REVIEW COMMITTEE
DATE: 12/10/97   SSA 5668
12/10
CA

Re NYairtel to Bureau dated 3/16/72.

Enclosed are 2 copies of a self-explanatory letter dated ███████ classified Secret. (S)

Bureau is requested to have the NYO fully identify the "International Committee for John and Yoko" (U)

Incorporate results in LHM.

CLASSIFIED BY: SSA 9803 RDO/JS   2/13/96
REASON: 1.5 (d) (b)
DECLASSIFY ON: X 6, X 5
CA# 83-1720

(U)

② - Bureau (2 encls)
1 - Foreign Liaison Desk
1 - London
WAK:rn
(4)

APPROPRIATE AGENCIES
AND FIELD OFFICES
ADVISED BY ROUTING
SLIP(S) OF _Class_

DATE 3.12.81

REC-52

EX-116 100 — 469910-22

REC-110

1B SEP 18 1972

9803 RDO/JS
7/2/92

CLASS. & EXT. BY ___
REASON FCIM II ___ 1-2.4.2 ___
DATE OF REVIEW ___ 9/12 ___

REG 18 SM LH 11 7/2/92 CA# 85-1720 1678

SAC MIAMI TO ACTING DIRECTOR FBI

September 28, 1972

Subject: John Winston Lennon

Security matter: RA (OO: New York)

Re New York airtel and LHM to Miami, July 27, 1972.

Copies of referenced LHM were disseminated to the Miami Beach Police Department in connection with the dissemination program in the MIDEM case. The Miami Beach Police Department and other local authorities have furnished no information to indicate the presence of the subject in Miami Beach, Florida, at any time during the summer of 1972.

The following informants were alerted concerning the subject but were unable to furnish information which would indicate his presence in Miami Beach: ***

On August 22, 1972, and August 23, 1972, approximately 1,200 individuals were arrested in Miami Beach by local authorities during protest demonstrations against the Republican National Convention. The records relating to these arrests were photographed by the Miami office and the film is currently being processed by the FBI Laboratory. When the arrest records become available, they will be reviewed to determine whether subject may have been arrested during the above conventions.

Memorandum

TO : ACTING DIRECTOR, FBI (100-469910) DATE: 9/28/72

FROM : SAC, MIAMI (100-16733) (P)

SUBJECT: JOHN WINSTON LENNON
SM - REVOLUTIONARY ACTIVITIES
(OO: NEW YORK)

Re New York airtel and LHM to Miami, 7/27/72.

Copies of referenced LHM were disseminated to
the Miami Beach Police Department in connection with
the dissemination program in the MIDEM case. The Miami
Beach Police Department and other local authorities
have furnished no information to indicate the presence
of the subject in Miami Beach, Florida, at any time
during the summer of 1972.

The following informants were alerted concerning the subject but were unable to furnish information which would indicate his presence in Miami
Beach: (X)(u)

b2
b7D

ALL INFORMATION CONTAINED
HEREIN IS UNCLASSIFIED EXCEPT
WHERE SHOWN OTHERWISE.

On 8/22/72 and 8/23/72 approximately 1,200
individuals were arrested in Miami Beach by local authorities
during protest demonstrations against the Republican
National Convention. The records relating to these arrests
were photographed by the Miami Office and the film is
currently being processed by the FBI Laboratory. When
the arrest records become available, they will be reviewed

② - Bureau (RM)
2 - New York (100-175319) (RM)
1 - Miami
WED/jah
(5)

REC 64

100-469910-2

EX OCT 2 1972

EX-117

57 OCT 3 1972 *Savings Bonds Regularly on the Payroll Savings Plan*

Transmit the following in _____

(Type in plaintext or code)

Via ___ AIRTEL _____

(Priority)

TO: ACTING DIRECTOR, FBI (100-469910)

FROM: SAC, NEW YORK (100-175319)(C)

SUBJECT: JOHN WINSTON LENNON
         SM - RA
         (OO:NY)

1678 RFP/KP 1-16.88
CLASS. BY 1678 RFP/EBM
4-6-83
Declass on

ReLegat, London letter, 9/12/72; NYlet, 8/30/72.

    Enclosed for the Bureau are ten copies of an LHM captioned "International Committee for John and Yoko," dated as above. Appropriate copies should be made available to Legat, London, as per their request. (u)

    In view of subject's inactivity in Revolutionary Activities and his seemingly rejection by NY Radicals, captioned case is being closed in the NY Division.

    In event other information comes to New York's attention indicating subject is active with Revolutionary groups, the case will be re-opened at that time and the Bureau advised accordingly.

    The Special Agent of the FBI who contacted INS was SA ████████████ b7C

2 - Bureau (RM) (Encls. 10)   SI-111
1 - New York

CJL:eps   REC-72   DATE 3-12-81

(4)   100-469910

ALL INFORMATION CONTAINED
HEREIN IS UNCLASSIFIED EXCEPT
WHERE SHOWN OTHERWISE.

11 DEC 11 1972

70 DEC 19 1972

Approved: _____   Sent _____ M Per _____
    Special Agent in Charge

☆U.S.Government Printing Office: 1972 — 455-57

SAC NEW YORK TO ACTING DIRECTOR FBI

December 8, 1972

Subject: John Winston Lennon

Security matter: RA (OO: NY)

ReLegat London letter September 12, 1972; NYlet August 30, 1972.

Enclosed for the Bureau are 10 copies of an LHM captioned 'International Committee for John and Yoko', dated as above. Appropriate copies should be made available to Legat, London, as per their request.

In view of subject's inactivity in revolutionary activities and his seemingly rejection by NY radicals, captioned case is being closed in the NY Division.

In event other information comes to New York's attention indicating subject is active with revolutionary groups, the case will be re-opened at that time and the Bureau advised accordingly.

The Special Agent of the FBI who contacted INS was SA ***.

Sources referred to in LHM are ***.

UNITED STATES DEPARTMENT OF JUSTICE – FBI, NEW YORK

December 8, 1972
Subject: International Committee for John and Yoko

On December 8, 1972, Mr Vincent Schiano, Chief Trial Attorney, Immigration and Naturalization Service, 20 West Broadway, New York City, New York, advised a representative of the Federal Bureau of Investigation that the 'International Committee for John and Yoko', has been established to campaign for John Winston Lennon and Yoko Ono Lennon who are currently appealing their deportation case in the United States.

> John Winston Lennon
> On February 2, 1972, Mr Raymond Connley, INS, New York City, advised that Lennon, Alien Registration Number A–17597321, first arrived in the United States through New York City on August 11, 1968, under a B–2 visitor's visa. He subsequently departed the United States and re-entered in 1971. Lennon is married to Yoko Ono Lennon, Alien Registration Number A–19489154. They both entered the United States together on August 13, 1971, and their visas were due to expire on February 29, 1972.

Mr Schiano further advised that the Lennons' deportation is still being appealed by their attorney.

During the months of September, October and November, 1972, sources of the FBI who are familiar with revolutionary type activities in the New York City area could not furnish additional information concerning this organization or the Lennons' activities.

Opposite Bed-in for peace, Amsterdam, March 1969
Overleaf Lennon on the set of *Help!*, 1965

1973—1980

DIRECTOR FBI TO SAC NEW YORK

September 19, 1973
Subject: John Winston Ono Lennon
           Board of Immigration Appeals

Enclosed for your office is one copy of Department of Justice memorandum dated September 18, 1973, requesting electronic surveillance information in accordance with specific questions set forth in the enclosed memorandum.

Conduct check in order to answer specific questions in enclosed memorandum and Criminal Division memorandum, April 16, 1969, furnished field May 2, 1969. Key answers to correspond with questions A through F. If results reveal positive information, insure microphone sources monitoring individuals involved are identified to the Bureau.

New York check captioned individual.

Sutel your response to reach Bureau by September 24, 1973. If positive, submit logs and pertinent documents by airtel.

One of 2,000 posters to appear in London and ten other cities in America, Europe and Japan as part of the Lennons' Christmas 1969 peace campaign

NEW YORK TO DIRECTOR FBI

September 21, 1973
Subject: ELSUR, John Winston Ono Lennon

ReBuairtel to New York, September 19, 1973

The special indices of the NYO and corresponding records were reviewed in accordance with Criminal Division memorandum dated April 16, 1969, concerning captioned individual, with the following results: (A) No; (B) No; (C-F) Not applicable.

Such a review failed to indicate that Lennon or premises in which he had proprietary interest have been subjected to any lawful electronic surveillance.

LENNON IS GIVEN 60 DAYS TO LEAVE
The New York Times, July 18, 1974

The Justice Department announced yesterday that John Lennon, the former Beatle, had been given 60 days to leave the country or be forcibly deported. The order is based on a decision reached by the Board of Immigration Appeals on July 10, and Mr Lennon's departure deadline is retroactive to that date.

Mr Lennon, who has been living in New York and other American cities since 1971, has fought lengthy and costly legal battles through the Immigration and Naturalization Service and the Federal courts to have his visa extended.

Extensions have been denied because he pleaded guilty in Britain, in 1968, to a charge of possession of marijuana. In his appeals of earlier denials of extensions Mr Lennon contended the marijuana had been planted in his home and he had pleaded guilty to the possession charge only to spare his former wife, then pregnant, the ordeal of a court appearance.

A spokesman for Mr Lennon's lawyer said that 'various avenues for appealing the order are being explored.'

WASHINGTON CAPITAL NEWS SERVICE

June 16, 1975

Night

New York (UPI): An attorney for former Beatle John Lennon said Monday that he has filed suit against former US Attorney General John N. Mitchell and others charging them with 'improper selective prosecution' in seeking to deport Lennon in 1972.

The attorney, Leon Wildes, said that in addition to Mitchell defendants in the Federal suit include the US Department of Justice, former Deputy Attorney General Richard G. Kleindienst and 'various immigration officers'.

The case is before Judge Richard Owen in Manhattan Federal Court.

Deportation proceedings against Lennon were started in New York in March, 1972. He was charged with overstaying his US visa, and prosecutors cited a 1968 British conviction for marijuana possession as the reason for denying him permanent residence.

At a news conference in 1973, New York Immigration Director Sol Marks said it was he who made the decision to proceed against Lennon.

Wildes said in a statement that he has obtained documents showing that Lennon's deportation was ordered from Washington on the strength of a Senate investigative report which sought to link the singer to a plan to disrupt the Republican National Convention in 1972.

WASHINGTON CAPITAL NEWS SERVICE

June 17, 1975

Day

New York (UPI): Former Beatle John Lennon, fighting a 1972 deportation order, has filed suit against the Justice Department, former Attorney General John N. Mitchell and other officials, charging they singled him out for 'improper selective prosecution'.

In 1973 New York Immigration Director Sol Marks said at a news conference he made the decision to proceed against Lennon himself.

Leon Wildes, Lennon's attorney, said Marks said in a deposition last week he acted as a 'conduit' for instructions from Washington, which he understood to mean that 'we were not to give this man a break'.

Marks also admitted he had misinformed the press at his 1973 news conference, Wildes said.

Wildes said Senator Strom Thurmond, R–S.C., sent a letter to Mitchell in February 1972, enclosing the committee memorandum.

'This appears to me to be an important matter, and I think it would be well to be considered at the highest level … as I can see many headaches might be avoided if appropriate action be taken in time', Wildes quoted Thurmond's letter as saying.

Wildes said other documents show Kleindienst sent the memo to Immigration Commissioner Raymond Farrell and that Farrell's deputy instructed subordinates in New York to seek deportation of Lennon and his wife, Yoko Ono.

Wildes said the suit names the Justice Department, Mitchell, Richard Kleindienst, deputy attorney general at the time and Mitchell's successor, and 'various immigration officers'.

RIDER TO APPLICATION FOR ADJUSTMENT OF STATUS
March 31, 1976

Re: John Winston Ono Lennon
Social Security 127–52–1582

Self-employment [over the past five years] was in connection with the following corporations:

Apple Corps, Limited
Maclen (Music) Limited
Lennon Productions Limited
Bag Productions, Limited
Joko Films, Limited
Subafilms, Limited
Apple Films, Limited
The Beatles, Limited
Lennon Productions, Inc.
Joko Films, Inc.
Bag Music Productions, Inc.
Yoko Ono Projects, Inc.
Ono Music, Inc.

(Signed)
John Winston Ono Lennon

Then this morning I went to the bookstore and bought *The Catcher in the Rye*. I'm sure the large part of me is Holden Caulfield, who is the main person in the book. The small part of me must be the Devil.

I went to the building. It's called the Dakota. I stayed there until he came out and asked him to sign my album. At that point my big part won and I wanted to go back to my hotel, but I couldn't. I waited until he came back. He came in a car. Yoko walked past first and I said hello, I didn't want to hurt her.

Then John came and looked at me and printed me. I took the gun from my coat pocket and fired at him. I can't believe I could do that. I just stood there clutching the book. I didn't want to run away. I don't know what happened to the gun. I remember Jose kicking it away. Jose was crying and telling me to please leave. I felt so sorry for Jose. Then the police came and told me to put my hands on the wall and cuffed me.

Statement of Mark David Chapman to police at 1 a.m.,
December 9, 1980, three hours after the murder of John Lennon

And I will not appeal any decision you have. If it's a decision to keep me here in the prison, I will not appeal it, and I never will. I'd like the opportunity to apologize to Mrs Lennon. I've thought about what it's like in her mind to be there that night, to see the blood, to hear the screams, to be up all night with the Beatle music playing through her apartment window. …

And there's something else I want to say. I feel that I see John Lennon now not as a celebrity. I did then. I saw him as a cardboard cut-out on an album cover. I was very young and stupid, and you get caught up in the media and the records and the music. And now I – I've come to grips with the fact that John Lennon was a person. This has nothing to do with being a Beatle or a celebrity or famous. He was breathing, and I knocked him right off his feet, and I don't feel because of that I have any right to be standing on my feet here, you know, asking for anything. I don't have a leg to stand on because I took his right out from under him, and he bled to death. And I'm sorry that ever occurred.

And I want to talk about Mrs Lennon again. I can't imagine her pain. I can't feel it. I've tried to think about what it would be like if somebody harmed my family, and there's just no way to make up for that, and if I have to stay in prison the rest of my life for that one person's pain, everybody else to the side for a second, just that one person's pain, I will. …

Again, I'm not saying these things for – for you to give me any kind of consideration for letting me go. I'm saying that because they are real, and it happened to me, and I felt her pain then, and I can honestly say I didn't want to feel it up until then. It's a horrible thing to, you know, realize what you've done.

Statement of Mark David Chapman to the New York Parole Board,
October 3, 2000

Moments of History

2002

The Irish Book of Death and Flying Ships

Marilyn Monroe: the FBI files

2003

The British War in Afghanistan

Escaping from Germany: the British Government files

The Great British Train Robbery, 1963

The Highland Division by Eric Linklater

John Lennon: the FBI files

The Mediterranean Fleet: Greece to Tripoli

The Scandal of Christine Keeler and John Profumo: Lord Denning's Report, 1963

The Shooting of John F. Kennedy, 1963: The Warren Commission

2004

Florence Nightingale

Nixon and Watergate

Peace in Tibet: the Younghusband expedition, 1904

Sacco and Vanzetti: the FBI files

The Theft of the Irish Crown Jewels, 1907

Victory in Europe, 1945: General Eisenhower's Report

War in Italy, 1944: the battles for Monte Cassino

Worldwide Battles of the Great War, 1915–1918

Uncovered Editions

Crime

Rillington Place, 1949

The Strange Story of Adolf Beck

The Trials of Oscar Wilde, 1895

Ireland
Bloody Sunday: Lord Widgery's Report, 1972
The Irish Uprising, 1914–21

Transport
The Loss of the Titanic, 1912
R.101: the Airship Disaster, 1930
Tragic Journeys (Titanic, R.101, Munich Air Crash)

Travel and British Empire
The Amritsar Massacre: General Dyer in the Punjab, 1919
The Boer War: Ladysmith and Mafeking, 1900
The British Invasion of Tibet: Colonel Younghusband, 1904
Florence Nightingale and the Crimea, 1854–55
King Guezo of Dahomey, 1850–52
Mr Hosie's Journey to Tibet, 1904
The Siege Collection (Kars, Boer War, Peking)
The Siege of Kars, 1855
The Siege of the Peking Embassy, 1900
Travels in Mongolia, 1902
Wilfred Blunt's Egyptian Garden: Fox-hunting in Cairo

Tudor History
Letters of Henry VIII, 1526–29

UK Politics since 1945
John Profumo and Christine Keeler, 1963
UFOs in the House of Lords, 1979
War in the Falklands, 1982

United States of America
The Assassination of John F. Kennedy, 1963
The Cuban Missile Crisis, 1962
The St Valentine's Day Massacre, 1929
UFOs in America, 1947
The Watergate Affair, 1972

The War Facsimiles

(Illustrated books published by the British government during the war years)
The Battle of Britain, August–October 1940
The Battle of Egypt, 1942
Bomber Command, September 1939–July 1941
East of Malta, West of Suez, September 1939 to March 1941
Fleet Air Arm, 1943
Land at War, 1939–1944
Ocean Front: the story of the war in the Pacific, 1941–1944
Roof over Britain, 1939–1942

World War I

British Battles of World War I, 1914–15
Defeat at Gallipoli: the Dardanelles Commission Part II, 1915–16
Lord Kitchener and Winston Churchill: the Dardanelles Commission Part I,
    1914–15
The Russian Revolution, 1917
War 1914: Punishing the Serbs
The World War I Collection (Dardanelles Commission, British Battles of World
    War I)

World War II

Attack on Pearl Harbor, 1941
D Day to VE Day: General Eisenhower's Report, 1944–45
Escape from Germany, 1939–45
The Judgment of Nuremberg, 1946
Tragedy at Bethnal Green
War 1939: Dealing with Adolf Hitler
The World War II Collection (War 1939, D Day to VE Day, Judgment of
    Nuremberg)
(see also *The War Facsimiles*)

UK Distribution and Orders

Littlehampton Book Services, Faraday Close, Durrington, West Sussex BN13 3RB
Telephone: 01903 828800 Fax: 01903 828801
E-mail: orders@lbsltd.co.uk

Sales Representation

Compass Independent Book Sales, Barley Mow Centre, 10 Barley Mow Passage,
Chiswick, London W4 4PH
Telephone: 0208 994 6477 Fax: 0208 400 6132

US Sales and Distribution

Midpoint Trade Books, 27 West 20th Street, Suite 1102, New York, NY 10011
Telephone: (1) 212 727 0190 Fax: (1) 212 727 0195

Midpoint Trade Books, 1263 Southwest Blvd, Kansas City, KS 66103
Telephone: (1) 913 831 2233 Fax: (1) 913 362 7401

Other Representation
Australia

Nick Walker, Australian Book Marketing/Australian Scholarly Publishing Pty Ltd
PO Box 299, Kew, Victoria 3101; Suite 102, 282 Collins Street, Melbourne 3000
Telephone: 03 9654 0250 Fax: 03 9663 0161
E-mail: aspec@ozemail.com.au

Scandinavia

Hanne Rotovnik, Publishers' Representative, PO Box 5, Strandvejen 785B,
DK-2930 Klampenborg
E-mail: Hanne@rotovnik.dk

South Africa

Colin McGee, Stephan Phillips (Pty) Ltd. PO Box 434, Umdloti Beach 4350
Telephone: +27 (0) 31 568 2902 Fax: +27 (0) 31 568 2922
E-mail: colinmcgee@mweb.co.za

Titles can also be ordered from www.timcoatesbooks.com